AWARD-WINNING CUSTOMER SERVICE

AWARD-WINNING CUSTOMER SERVICE

101 Ways to Guarantee Great Performance

Renée Evenson

AMACOM

New York • Atlanta • Brussels * Chicago • Mexico City
San Francisco • Shanghai • Tokyo • Washington, D. C.

Special discounts on bulk quantities of AMACOM books are available to corporations, professional associations, and other organizations. For details, contact Special Sales Department, AMACOM, a division of American Management Association, 1601 Broadway, New York, NY 10019.
Tel.: 212-903-8316. Fax: 212-903-8083.
Web site: www. amacombooks.org

Library of Congress Cataloging-in-Publication Data

Evenson, Renée
Award-winning customer service : 101 ways to guarantee great performance / by Renée Evenson.
p. cm.
Includes bibliographical references and index.
ISBN-13: 978-0-8144-7454-9
ISBN-10: 0-8144-7454-3
1. Customer services. 2. Customer relations. 3. Employees—Training of. I. Title.
HF5415.5.E885 2007
658.8′12—dc22

2007008289

Printing number

10 9 8 7 6 5 4 3 2 1

This book is dedicated to my husband, Joe,
who is always here for me.
You are my rock.

And to my parents, Don and Rose, who taught me
to believe in myself and to always strive to achieve my best.

A special note of gratitude for . . .
My wonderful family who brings me so much happiness,
My menagerie of kitties who love me no matter what,
All of my good friends who love me no matter what!

I am thankful for each and every one of you.

CONTENTS

ACNOWLEDGMENTS

A special note of appreciation to the following people; each of you helped me to be a better writer during the process of completing this book:

My agent, Michael Snell, thank you for your guidance. Your suggestions are always on target.

My editor, Ellen Kadin, I greatly appreciate your continued support. Your constructive and heartfelt comments are always welcome.

My copyeditors, Barbara Chernow and associates. I've learned so much from you.

My associate editor, Mike Sivilli. Your behind-the-scenes input helped make production smooth.

My proofreaders, Rose Aschbrenner and Joseph Balka—I pay close attention to your honest feedback. Thank you for your time and your input on this book.

My clients—I listen carefully to you. Thank you for your loyalty.

INTRODUCTION

Why do customers take their business elsewhere? Some move away. Some change because they are not satisfied with the product. Some go for competitive reasons. But the majority of customers take their business elsewhere because of an indifferent attitude toward them by the business owner, manager, or frontline employee. Most of the time these customers don't even complain. They just don't come back.

Do you know the key factors that cause customer dissatisfaction? Research has discovered that the top reasons for customer dissatisfaction focus specifically on employees who: don't listen to what the customer is saying; ignore customers completely; don't do what they say they will when they say they will; aren't knowledgeable about their company's products and services; and don't follow up or follow through.

Providing consistently high-quality service puts you and your company on the fast track to success. How well you treat your customers may make the difference between achieving your business goals and just barely keeping your doors open (or not keeping them open at all!). Giving great customer service is not a matter of doing *what you think* your customers want. Rather, it is a matter of doing *what* your customers want. One of the greatest mistakes business owners make is assuming they know what their customers want without actually asking the customers what they want. To understand customers, you need to get close to them, stay tuned in to them, and think like them. Frontline employees are your key to success. They present the face of your business to the world, so it is crucial that you train them to interact effectively with customers.

Most business managers, owners, and employees understand the importance of great customer service, but they often lack the skills and knowledge to know how to handle all situations. Although you understand how important customers are, you may have coworkers who do not appreciate their importance. Managers and team leaders will often ignore employee behavior problems because they simply do not know how to deal with them. The sad news is that ignoring problems will not make them go away. Rather, ignoring them may make customers go away.

Customer service is the most important aspect of your job. You get it. How can you get all your coworkers to get it?

Customer service leaders need a practical tool to help them learn the skills necessary to train employees and transform problem behavior. This book offers a whole set of attitude adjustment tools, tips, and helpful advice for problem-solving issues of providing customer service. Written for the busy person with little time to search for solutions, this book provides the necessary skills for learning and teaching coworkers how to give exceptional customer service.

Seasoned employees will appreciate brushing up on these helpful tips, while new employees will find it a handy training tool. Thus, all employees will find the book relevant and helpful. Each page is packed with valuable information, including practical examples of what to say when encountering delicate business situations.

Every day we play different roles. We play one role when we parent our children, and another when we socialize with friends. At work, we play a different role altogether. Changing our mindset to adjust to each role is important if we are to play each part to the best of our ability. Customer service is a role some people choose, yet many do not know how to interact well with patrons.

Leading customer service employees to perform their best is like directing actors in a play. First, you find a good script. Second, you cast the correct actors for the roles. Third, you ensure everyone learns the lines. Fourth, you rehearse. Finally, you are ready for opening night. Unless you execute each of these steps correctly, your play might not have a second night. Do everything to delight your audience, and you will receive rave reviews. How successfully you acted and directed are ultimately decided by the audience, so it is important to spend time becoming acquainted with your audience.

The play director analogy is used throughout this book. Each chapter begins by relating an aspect of a director's role in putting on a great performance. The common theme throughout the book is that everyone is in charge of his or her own performance; therefore everyone should think like a director. Similarly, every director is a cast member, who needs to know how to perform each role well. In other words, managers and employees are responsible for their own behavior.

The most important benefits of learning the tips in this book are increased productivity, efficiency, and job satisfaction. It is cheaper and faster when your frontline employees do the job right the first time. Changing the attitude of an unhappy customer costs a lot more, both in dollars and time, than satisfying that customer from the beginning. Finally, learning how to communicate well, how to positively interact with others, and how to become a strong leader will help you, not only on the job, but in *all* areas of your life.

Can you afford NOT to read this book? Not if you want to be your customers' number one choice.

AWARD-WINNING CUSTOMER SERVICE

CHAPTER 1

CUSTOMERS
Delight Your Audience

"I don't believe in elitism. I don't think the audience is this dumb person lower than me. I am the audience."
—QUENTIN TARANTINO

You are thrilled that you were able to get tickets for the opening night of a new play. You are an actor and enjoy seeing an exciting new production. As the curtain rises, you scan the stage, noting the set and actors. The actors begin moving about. One actress forgets her first line. One of the other actors cues her, and the play gets underway. Soon another actor flubs his lines. Others in the cast don't seem to know their moves, and they bump into each other. Most of the actors speak so softly they're barely audible. Someone in the audience calls to them to speak up, but they ignore the comment. The mumbling and bumbling continue and, by the end of the first act, you wonder how much time the cast spent rehearsing. The play continues to go downhill. As the second act ends, people in the audience boo, groan, and complain. Some leave before the third act begins. By the end of the play, it's obvious that the actors and director don't have a clear understanding of what it takes to put on a production. Even though the props and stage setting were good, that wasn't enough for the audience to give it a good review.

This should never happen in the production of any play. By opening night, the cast should be so well rehearsed that a decent performance comes naturally. You could forgive some minor mistakes, but it is difficult to imagine that a director would send the cast on stage without thoroughly rehearsing. It just would not happen, would it?

Why, then, does it happen in business? Managers send their employees out to serve their most important audience—their customers—without ensuring they know how to put on a decent production. Like the audience members who left before the third act, your customers will leave in the middle of your performance unless you give them what they need.

In the theater world, it is all about the audience. Audience members buy the tickets that keep plays running. In business, it is all about the customers, who buy the goods and keep your doors open. Unlike an audience whose members will boo and voice their opinions, most customers will not express their complaints. They will just take their business somewhere else. Unless you recognize problem areas and correct employee behavior, you will lose business. The first step to exceptional customer service is awareness. The leading reasons for customer dissatisfaction are employees who ignore customers, don't listen, aren't knowledgeable, aren't reliable, and don't follow up or follow through.

To put on your best performance, pay attention to your audience; know your lines; do what you say you will when you say you will; and follow up. You should perform these steps correctly, because you might not get a second chance. Do everything to delight your audience, and you will put on an award winning production.

"I can't deny the fact that you like me! You like me!"

—SALLY FIELD

1. Pay Attention

Have you ever walked into a business and been completely ignored by the employees? Most likely the answer is yes. When it happened, you probably felt invisible. You may have even walked out wondering how a company can stay in business when its employees treat customers as if they were nonexistent. When employees make customers feel invisible, they might actually become invisible.

Performance Prompts

- Stop whatever you are doing when a customer comes in or calls.
- Greet the customer, and give your name.
- Ask how you can help.
- Look directly at the customer.
- Focus only on the customer you are helping.
- Make eye contact and smile to show your positive attitude.
- During phone calls, let your smile come through your voice.
- Stay interested.
- Do what you can to help each customer.
- Show rather than point or tell.
- Never accept a personal call while assisting a customer.
- Always give customers more than they expect.

When This Happens . . .

You and your coworkers are responsible for stocking shelves and setting up window displays. Sometimes, you become so involved in these tasks that you do not notice when customers enter your store. When you do notice them, you really prefer to continue what you are doing. You joke with your coworkers that customers can be a real pain when they interrupt your "real" work.

Try This

Ouch! You and your coworkers need an attitude adjustment. Nothing is more important than helping your customers. Stocking shelves and setting up window displays are important, but the mindset that these tasks are your most important jobs can be dangerous. If customers stop coming, you will not need to stock the shelves. If you do not sell the merchandise, your business is going to close. No matter what you are doing, your customers *are* your most important job. Stop! And pay attention to them.

The customer is the reason you have a job.

2. Listen Carefully to Your Customers

Paying attention and listening go hand in hand. If you do not pay attention, you cannot be a good listener, and if you do not listen well, you are not paying attention. Did you ever speak to someone who was not listening to you? It can be upsetting, especially when you have to repeat yourself for no apparent reason. When communicating, speaking well is important, but listening well is even more important. If you do not listen well, you will not know how to respond appropriately. You are in the customer service business and listening to your customers matters to them. It matters a lot.

Performance Prompts

- Ask how you can help, and then listen to the answer.
- Form the mindset that this one customer is the reason you have a job.
- You cannot listen and talk at the same time, so keep quiet and listen when the customer is talking.
- Listen actively and completely.
- Listen for what is not said. Pay attention to the nonverbal clues and tone of voice.
- Remain objective and never judge a customer based on appearance or manner of speaking.
- Before responding or forming your conclusion, gather as much information as you need to make sure you understand the customer's needs and concerns.

When This Happens . . .

You notice that your coworker, Steven, is easily distracted when he talks to customers. He looks toward the door every time someone comes in, even when he is already helping a customer. Customers frequently have to repeat themselves because he does not listen. Today you heard a customer make a negative comment about Steven on the way out.

Try This

Talk to Steven about this. As your coworker, he is equally responsible for satisfying customers. Tell him what the customer said and that you have seen him behave inattentively with other customers. If he does not understand, show him what you mean. As he talks, continually look away, as though you are distracted. Ask him to repeat what he said. Then remind him that this is how he treats his customers.

Listen actively—focus entirely on your customer.

3. Know Your Business

A fairly basic concept for employees in customer service is that you should know your business. Do you? Are you completely knowledgeable about all that your company has to offer? To find the best solution for your customers' problems, you need to know what the best solution is.

Performance Prompts

- Learn all you can about your products and services, as well as those of your competitors.
- Learn about your entire company operation.
- Always search for the best solution for your customer.
- Be a problem solver, not part of the problem.
- Be prepared to offer an alternative solution if the customer is not satisfied with your first option.
- Effectiveness is important to customers. To be effective, you must be knowledgeable.
- Efficiency is important to customers. To be efficient, you must be productive.
- Finding the right solution, but taking too long, is as ineffective as handling the customer's request quickly, but not finding the right solution.
- Strive to balance effectiveness and efficiency by finding the right solution as quickly as you can.

When This Happens . . .

You consider yourself knowledgeable about your products and services. After all, you feel comfortable describing particular products to customers and telling them where to locate them in your store. Take the example of Mr. Barkley, a frequent customer at your home supply store who asks if you carry a new type of glue he saw advertised on television.

Try This

Knowing your products and services requires more than a descriptive response about a particular item. If you answer Mr. Barkley by saying, "Yes, that's a new extra strength glue that just came out. Let me show you where it's located," he will be satisfied. You told him you carry it, described it, and showed him where to find it. Imagine if you answered Mr. Barkley by asking, "Yes, we have that. It's a new extra strength glue that just came out. What are you going to use it for?" When he says he needs to glue a china dish he broke, you say, "that glue isn't made for porous items like china. We do have another product that will work well. In fact, I've used it myself successfully at home." When you take the time to ask, customers will take the time to talk. Their answers may clue you into a better solution. Had Mr. Barkley left with the glue he asked about, he would be dissatisfied when the product failed to work as he expected.

Ask questions. Pay attention, and listen to the customer's answer. Being knowledgeable about your business means finding the right solution for each customer's need. That is the best way to satisfy your customers.

Learn your job well.

4. Do What You Say You Will When You Say You Will

You might feel you give great customer service, but unless you do what you say you will when you say you will, your customers are only going to remember that you were not reliable or dependable. They will forget about the great customer service you gave them up to that point.

Performance Prompts

- Always do what you say you will when you say you will. Period.
- If you make a commitment, make sure you meet it.
- When you need to get back to your customer, make a commitment you can keep. Think about the length of time you need to resolve the problem and make your commitment accordingly.
- Customers would rather have you commit to a realistic time frame than a time frame that sounds good but is unrealistic.
- If you made a commitment that you cannot meet, call your customer and explain the delay. Most customers are understanding as long as you are honest with them.
- When making commitments, never answer "as soon as possible" or "right away." These time frames mean one thing to you, but they probably mean something different to your customer.
- Always give a definite commitment. Say, "I'll get back to you by five on Friday," rather than, "I'll call you back when I have the answer."

When This Happens . . .

Ms. Robbins is upset with your company. She received an order this morning with two incorrect items. You told her you will check what happened and get back to her by five today with a resolution. She angrily says, "I need these items, and I want an answer within an hour." You know you need more time to find out what went happened and devise the best solution.

Try This

Ms. Robbins is already upset, so choose your words carefully. You do not want to upset her further. "Ms. Robbins, I'd like to be able to call you back within the hour, but I need time to research what happened and find out how quickly we can get the correct products to you. I don't want to tell you I'll call you back within an hour when I know I won't have my answer within that time frame. I'm going to work on this immediately, and I will definitely call you back with a resolution by five today." Ms. Robbins will appreciate your confident and honest reply.

Reliability and dependability are important to customers.

5. Follow Up for Satisfaction

Most likely, you will not need to follow up every customer contact, but there are situations in which a follow up is appropriate. In the case of a customer who is upset with your company, like Ms. Robbins, a follow up is not only appropriate, it should be standard procedure.

Performance Prompts

- Follow up to make sure your customer knows how to use a new product.
- Follow up if your customer had a lot of questions before buying the product.
- Follow up if the customer was confused about the agreed-upon solution to a problem.
- Follow up to thank a customer for a large sale.
- Follow up by telling existing customers about new products or an upcoming sale.
- Follow up when a customer is upset with your company. After finding the best solution to the problem, follow up to make sure the customer is satisfied.

When This Happens . . .

You research what happened with Ms. Robbins's order and call her back around three with an answer. "Ms. Robbins, I called our ordering department and found out what happened. Two of the product numbers were transposed. I'm really sorry this happened. We do have the correct items in stock and are shipping them to you overnight at no charge. They will be delivered tomorrow morning. We are also including a return label for you to send the incorrect items back." Ms. Robbins thanks you. She appears to be satisfied.

Try This

In this situation, a follow up is warranted, so make a note to call Ms. Robbins around noon tomorrow to make sure the items were delivered. "Ms. Robbins, this is Jamie from Rock's Home Supply. I'm calling to make sure the items were delivered this morning." WOW. Ms. Robbins is impressed that you took the time to call. If, for some reason, the items were not delivered as promised, you headed her off at the pass and saved another angry phone call to your company. Let's assume, however, that she received her order. She is now completely satisfied that you resolved her problem and pleasantly surprised that you took the time to call and check.

Follow up any time you feel customer satisfaction is at stake.

6. Making Customers Happy Is Job #1

The customer is the reason you have a job. You are in the customer service business, and this should be your mantra. You may also want to add to your mantra that *without customers, customer service employees are not needed.*

You have learned the most common reasons for customer dissatisfaction are employees who ignore customers, don't listen, aren't responsible, aren't knowledgeable, and don't follow up. You also learned that most of the time, customers will not even complain. They just will not come back. The only way for you to know if you are making customers happy is to always stay on top of your game.

Performance Prompts

- You present the face of your business, so learn how to present yourself properly at all times.
- Your coworkers look to your entire team and your manager to set the level of expectation. Whatever you are willing to accept is what you are going to get, so set the bar high.
- Do not anticipate what customers need. Ask them what they need.
- Ask what you are doing right and what you can do to improve. Then, tune in to customers' replies.
- Make sure customers are important to you. If they are important to you, they will be important to your coworkers.
- Always stay tuned in to your customers—and to your coworkers—to stay one step ahead of the crowd.

None of this is rocket science. Giving high quality customer service is really very simple. It begins—and ends—with your commitment to your customers. Learn how to do your job well. Expect the best from yourself and from your coworkers. Nothing less is acceptable for you to build a strong and loyal customer base.

When This Happens . . .

Mrs. Jones just pulled into your parking lot. She is a customer who complains about everything. Your coworkers start making wise cracks and derogatory comments about her. They jokingly say that you will have to handle her.

Try This

You feel the same about Mrs. Jones, so it would be easy to join your coworkers in making jokes. Don't. If you joke or talk negatively about a customer, it gives them the green light to do the same. Show your coworkers that you are above making fun of your customers. Say something like, "Hey Guys, Mrs. Jones does a lot of business here. We don't know anything about her personal situation, so let's help her without judging her." Then step up to the plate and show your coworkers how to give exceptional customer service, even to one of your most difficult customers. When your coworkers see how you treat Mrs. Jones, they will be less likely to make fun of her in the future.

Remember, the customer is the reason you have a job. Without customers, customer service employees are not needed.

CHAPTER 2

PERFORMANCE

Your Role of a Lifetime

"With any part you play, there is a certain amount of yourself in it. There has to be, otherwise it's just not acting. It's lying."

—JOHNNY DEPP

Yesterday's newspaper ran an ad for an open casting call for a new play that will be opening in your city. You decide to audition for a role—any role. You've done some acting previously, you even directed before, so you feel confident that you will be selected. After all the auditions, the producers announce that you are cast as a frontline employee in this play called *Customer Service*. You are happy that you won a part, even though you don't quite understand your role or how it relates to the entire play. You also aren't sure if you are ready for a frontline role, but you are confident that after you read the entire script you will be prepared to play your role well. One of the producers assures the cast that the play has no minor roles. Every role is important. Each character is part of the cast, and it is the cast that puts on the production. Everyone must work together as a cohesive group if the production is to succeed. If one person is ineffective, the play can flop.

After hearing the producer's speech, you feel better about the role you were cast to play. You are convinced that no matter what your role, you can be a star. It is all in your mindset. You remind yourself that all legendary actors started someplace. Few started their careers in lead roles. They rose to stardom because they shone in every role. You picture yourself shining in this role so that you, too, can rise to stardom.

When you enter the door to your workplace each day, remember that you are an actor in the play called *Customer Service*. Get into your character. Whether you are a manager or a frontline employee, you need to be in charge of your performance. No one can make you a star. Only you can do that because you direct your behavior. Every actor is a director—and—every director is an actor. Every employee is a manager—and every manager is an employee. You are the manager of you.

If it is difficult to think of yourself as an actor in the customer service production, consider that you play many roles in your life. Every day, you move in and out of different characters. At home, you may play the role of parent. You have the lead role in that scene, but your role changes if you visit your parents. You may be the star on your softball team, but if you move out of your comfort zone by joining a soccer team, you will be relegated to a minor role until you prove your worth. Socialize with friends, and you assume a different character than when you are at work.

Remember that everyone with a role in the play of customer service is part of the whole cast. And the cast puts on the production. Think of your customers as your audience. No matter your role, give them the performance of your life. Lead the way by consistently giving exceptional service. Be the star of your production.

"I think it's always best to be who you are."

—HALLE BERRY

7. Present Your Best Face Forward

In face-to-face situations, people see you first and hear you second. When people see you for the first time, they quickly size you up and begin forming their first impression. At work, your appearance tells your customers, manager, and coworkers who you are and what you think about yourself. Work is not the place for a radical or extreme statement. Cleansing, grooming, and dressing properly may take a little extra time but the pay off is worth it. When you look good, you feel good about yourself.

Performance Prompts

- At work, dress professionally. When you look professional, you will act professionally.
- Dress appropriately for your work environment. Work is not the place to stand out in the crowd.
- If you are uncertain how to dress, stay on the conservative side.
- You do not have to spend a fortune on business clothes to dress professionally. How much the clothes cost is not important; how they look is important.
- Make sure you are clean before you leave home. Take a shower, wash your hair, scrub your fingernails, and brush your teeth.
- Make sure you are groomed before you leave home. Style your hair, wear wrinkle-free clothes, file your fingernails, and shine your shoes.
- Look in a full-length mirror before you leave home. If you do not have one, buy one. A full-length mirror is a good investment.
- Check yourself during the day. Also, ask a close friend or coworker to tell you when something is amiss with your appearance.

- Select your outfit the night before to avoid the morning rush or any surprises. When you are rushed, you might not choose wisely.

When This Happens . . .

Tomorrow is your first day on a new job. You will be a frontline customer service employee in a call center. You are excited about this new job, but you do not have a clue what to wear.

Try This

Tomorrow you will make a first impression with your new coworkers, as well as with your manager. Think about how your manager dressed during your interview. If you took a tour of the call center, think about how the employees were dressed. If you still have no clue what to wear, select something conservative. A pair of dress slacks and a nice sweater or shirt should suffice for your first day. Rule out anything loud or faddish until you have time to size up your new office environment. Plan to wake up a little early to allow for personal hygiene and grooming. Tomorrow morning you will most likely feel a little nervous, and you do not want any last minute surprises.

Looking good—appropriate for your environment—
can help boost your confidence.

8. Maintain a Positive Attitude

The best thing you can do for yourself, not to mention for others, is to always maintain a positive attitude. No matter how you feel inside, present a positive face to the world. It goes a long way. When you concentrate on being positive, you will feel more positive. You view the world differently when you view it from a positive perspective. Think about it: What type of people would you rather be around—those who lift you up or those who drag you down?

Performance Prompts

- Attitude is everything. Good or bad!
- Your attitude is what your customers will remember.
- You may not get a second chance to impress someone.
- Smile. A smile goes a long way. When you smile at others, they smile back. Try it. It works.
- Appreciate every day.
- Feel grateful. You are where you are for a reason. Appreciate all that you have in this place, at this time.
- Develop an empathetic nature. Putting yourself in another person's shoes helps you look at the situation from a different perspective.
- Focus on the present. You cannot change the past, and you cannot predict the future. All you have is now.
- Stay interested. One of the best ways to show others you have a positive frame of mind is to stay focused on them.
- Believe that you can make a difference. This begins with believing in yourself.

When This Happens . . .

You are having a problem at home that is dragging you down at work. Although you do not like to talk about it, you sense that your bad moods are rubbing off on your coworkers.

Try This

We all carry emotional baggage. Face it: Everyone has problems. If you think that yours are worse than those of other people, you are looking at your situation only from your own perspective. Make a conscious effort to leave your emotional baggage outside the office door. Never make your customers and coworkers suffer because you have a problem. Besides, putting your problems aside for a few hours may help. You might be able to look at things from a different perspective and maintain a positive attitude at work.

It is all in your presentation. ALL!

9. Exude Confidence

Many confident people are made, not born. Yes, that is correct. Not all confident people were born that way. Confidence is a trait that can be developed. If you develop confidence, you can change your entire demeanor and find ways to shine in every role you play.

Performance Prompts

- The first step in developing confidence is to create in your mind a positive vision of the person you wish to become.
- If you have trouble seeing that vision of yourself clearly, take time to focus on the qualities you want to personify and begin to envision the *"you"* you want to be.
- Keep this vision in your consciousness.
- Change your self-talk to reflect the new you. Envision yourself as a confident person. Tell yourself that you are confident and self-assured. Picture yourself exuding confidence.
- Act confidently. In the beginning, you will have to force yourself out of your comfort zone by acting confidently even when you do not feel confident.
- Acting confidently does not mean being someone you are not. It does mean presenting yourself in a more self-assured manner. With practice, you will find that you no longer have to act confident because you will have become a more confident person.
- Dress for success. When you look good, you will feel good.
- Remember that it is up to you to sell yourself. No one can do that better than you.
- Selling yourself does not mean bragging. Rather, it means putting your best face forward and showcasing your good qualities.
- Always focus on your best qualities.

When This Happens . . .

Today you are starting a new job in the customer service department. You were promoted because of your ability to work well with others and your knowledge of the company's products and services. You wake up with a huge knot in your stomach. You feel as though all your confidence has been sucked out of you.

Try This

Focus on the positives. Think: *I deserve this promotion because of my job knowledge, because I consistently give exceptional customer service, and because of my ability to work well with my coworkers. I am good at what I do.* Next, picture yourself interacting with your customers and coworkers and presenting yourself as confident and capable. Tell yourself: *I get along well with others, and my coworkers respect me.* When your confidence wanes and you begin negative self-talk, immediately tell yourself to stop, change your self-talk to positive thoughts, and envision yourself handling your new duties with confidence.

Believe in yourself.

10. Honesty Is Always Your Best Choice

When you make a habit of always telling the truth and doing the right thing, life becomes less complicated. When you tell the truth, you do not have to remember what lies you said to whom. When you are dishonest, people find out. Maybe not right away, but the truth always has a way of coming out. When people find that you have been dishonest, they will no longer trust you.

Performance Prompts

- Always be honest. Period.
- In situations where honesty is going to hurt someone, saying nothing may be the best policy. You are not lying. Rather, you are protecting someone's feelings.
- Do the right thing. Think before making decisions to be sure that what you are doing is right and ethical.
- Do what you say you will when you say you will. Become a person others can rely on.
- When you give someone your word, mean it. Let your word be your bond.
- Never knock your competition. You will be the one who looks bad.
- Always be truthful about your products, services, and policies. Never make misleading claims.
- Be accountable for your actions. When you make a mistake, be up front and admit it. When you take responsibility for your actions, people will respect you.

When This Happens . . .

Sally, a great employee and your close friend, is telling everyone she is being promoted to a position in Frank's department, but Frank told you he is promoting someone else. He knows that Sally is a great employee, but there is something about her he just does not like. He cannot put his finger on it, but a promotion for Sally is not happening.

Try This

Telling Sally that Frank does not like her would be hurtful, but so is allowing her to continue telling people she is getting a promotion when she is not, particularly if she finds out you knew she was not. Say this: "Sally, Frank told me that he's decided to promote someone else. I know you are a great employee, and I believe in your abilities. I'm sure another opportunity will come up." You did not sugar coat the situation, and you did not lie. If Sally asks you if you know the reason she is not getting the promotion, you could say, "Frank told me he knows you are a great employee, but he doesn't feel you are the right person to work in his department." You protected her feelings by telling her a kind version of the details.

Do everything with integrity. Everything.

11. Energize Yourself

Keeping your energy level steady throughout the day helps you perform consistently rather than seesawing between highs and lows. Food is your body's fuel, and what you eat is important in maintaining a consistent energy level. Exercise boosts your energy level, and sleep is your rejuvenator. Eating well, exercising, and getting enough sleep are key to maintaining high energy.

Performance Prompts

- Breakfast is the most important meal of the day. You heard this before, and you heard correctly.
- Your body needs refueling in the morning and throughout the day with healthy and nutritious food.
- Include whole grains, protein, fruit, vegetables, and low or no-fat dairy products in your daily diet.
- You can still eat nutritiously, even when on the run. Grab a piece of fruit, a whole grain muffin, a yogurt, a handful of nuts. . . .
- Balance, moderation, and variety are important to your nutrition.
- Control fat and sugar intake.
- Incorporate regular exercise into your daily plan.
- Park away from your office, and walk.
- Take the stairs rather than riding the elevator.
- When you start feeling drowsy, stand up, stretch, walk, or take deep breaths to pump up your energy level.
- When you eat a healthy diet, exercise, and get enough sleep every day, you will receive psychological benefits by decreasing stress and tension.

When This Happens . . .

Getting up, getting the kids and yourself ready for the day, making sure everyone eats breakfast, getting out of the house and to school and work on time . . . picking the kids up from school, running errands, running the kids to soccer practice, eating a rushed dinner, making sure the kids do their homework, getting them ready for bed, falling into bed from exhaustion. With such a schedule, you have no time for you. Does this sound similar to your day? Even if you do not have kids or all of these responsibilities, you most likely still live a rushed life. Fast forwarding through life has become part of our culture. The bottom line is that you probably feel you are far too busy—and stressed out—to worry about eating right. And exercise? Forget about that. You have no time.

Try This

Make time! That is the bottom line. If you do not make time to eat a healthy diet, exercise, and sleep, your body is not going to receive the fuel and energy it needs to keep going. You will go through each day too exhausted to enjoy life. You will eventually run out of fuel and become ill. So, replace unhealthy foods with healthier choices. You will feel better. Get enough sleep. You will feel better. Schedule time every day to exercise. You will feel better. Do all these things, and you are taking a huge step toward feeling great.

Schedule time for you every day.

12. Bounce Back with Resiliency

Resiliency is one of the most important qualities you can possess. Resilient people bounce back from life's challenges, learn how to overcome difficult situations, hold up under pressure, and find renewed strength in their experiences. Like confident people, resilient people are not born with this quality. Like confidence, resiliency can be developed.

Performance Prompts

- When life throws you a curve, do not complain about how unfair your situation is.
- Put your problem-solving skills to work, and find the best solution.
- When there is no good solution, deal with the problem to the best of your ability.
- Sometimes biding your time is the only good solution. Remind yourself that in time the situation will look different.
- Draw on your inner strength to get you through the really tough times.
- Learning a life lesson from your experiences helps you deal with the next curve that comes your way.
- Lower your expectations about outcomes. When you expect less, you are less likely to be devastated by curves.
- When you lower your expectations, you will become more flexible. Flexible people are also adaptable people. In today's fast-forward world, adaptability is a welcome trait.
- Try to maintain balance in your life. When you are going through tough times, eating healthy foods and exercising can boost your immunity. Doing these two things can also keep you from becoming depressed.
- Most importantly, keep your sense of humor. Laughter really is the best medicine.

When This Happens . . .

You feel devastated because you just found out your father is in the early stages of Alzheimer's disease. As the only child living close to him, you know that you will become his primary caregiver. You do not know how you are going to juggle this with your home and work responsibilities—and do a good job at either.

Try This

Life has thrown you a curve. You naturally feel a sense of despair because you are already grieving the loss of the father you know. Is this unfair? Yes, it is unfair. But if you focus on the unfairness of your situation, you will be unable to move forward. Instead, you should move into a problem-solving mode. Analyze the situation. Try to be objective. Think of the best solution for caring for your father, while still taking care of your other responsibilities. Cut out the nonessential things in your life right now. It is critical that you eat a healthy diet, make time to exercise, and, most importantly, make time to laugh and have some fun. Talk to people who will understand.

Always try to make lemonade out of lemons,
even if you can only squeeze out a drop.

CHAPTER 3

PLANNING

A Good Script Begins with Thoughtful Consideration

"Luck is where opportunity meets preparation."

—DENZEL WASHINGTON

Today is your first rehearsal. After studying your lines, you still don't quite understand your character. Still, you are confident that you'll have a better feel for the role after today's rehearsal. Bob, the director, begins by telling you about himself. He has acted in the *Customer Service* play before and received good reviews for his performance. That's why he was asked to direct this play. He asks the cast to read through the play. As you do, he sits quietly, saying nothing. After one run through, he says he is satisfied with the way everyone is getting into character, schedules the next rehearsal, and assures all of you that after one more rehearsal, you will be ready for opening night. You now understand your role better, but Bob did nothing to pull the cast together. On the way out, you and some of the other actors share your concern about Bob's inability to direct. He doesn't seem to have a clear vision about the direction of the play, he offered no advice, and it's clear that he hasn't even planned the wardrobe, set design, or props. What should you do? Do you continue to moan and groan with the other actors or do you share your concerns with Bob before this play heads south?

After reminding yourself what the producer said at your audition, you decide to talk to Bob. Every actor is part of the cast, and it is the entire cast that will make this production a success or doom it to be a one night stand. Unless Bob drastically changes his directing style, this play has no chance. Even though Bob had acted previously, he underestimated how different it would be to direct.

Directing involves a lot more than getting the actors together and making sure everyone knows their lines. Directing includes preparing for a smooth production by formulating a mission, writing a plan, setting realistic goals, and measuring results to stay on track. Actors rely on directors to share the mission, plan, and goals with them, as well as to explain their roles in the production.

Employees, like actors, look to their leaders for direction and an explanation of their roles in providing exceptional customer service. They follow their leaders' cues. To give the best customer service, you must formulate your mission, write a customer focused plan, and set relevant goals that move you toward fulfilling your mission. Then, you must track and measure results to monitor your team's progress.

Because you are your own manager, step outside of yourself and look at the big picture. You can either complain about the way things are, or you can help improve the situation. If you want to be a customer service star, analyze your role and what you can do to accomplish your company's mission. Think about the ways you can give exceptional service to your customers. Devise your own personal mission that incorporates your role, formulate your plan, and set goals that map out your personal path to success.

"And also it's a little bit of, the more they say,
'No, you can't,' the more you say,
'No, you know what? Yes, I can.' "

—CHARLIZE THERON

13. Create a Personal Mission Statement

Without a written mission statement, it is easy to lose your way. Think about this. You and your family decide to take a vacation, so you pack your bags, load them into your car, and take off for your vacation. Because you do not have a clear destination in mind, you drive down one road until someone in the backseat tells you to turn down another. You turn on to that road, then someone else pipes in that it is a boring road. Soon everyone is arguing about which road to take. You return home exhausted, having spent your entire vacation driving aimlessly because you did not have a destination.

A mission statement is your destination. It tells, in exact words, what your company stands for and what you wish to achieve. Having a mission statement provides everyone in your organization with a clear focus and, most importantly, the same focus.

Performance Prompts

- Begin by analyzing what you, your company, and your team stand for.
- What service or product do you provide? Why is it important to your customers, and what is your role in providing that service or selling that product?
- What level of performance do you expect from yourself?
- How do you expect your customers to be treated?
- Your mission statement should be very specific about what your company (or you) expects to achieve.
- Your mission statement should be brief.
- Post your company and personal mission statements for your team and coworkers to see. Make sure each statement is clear, so everyone understands it.
- Focus daily on your mission.
- Everything you do should in some way move you toward your destination.

When This Happens...

You do not see the need to write out a mission statement because you already have a clear vision of your company's goals and the personal values by which you operate. After all, your company has a mission statement that is posted. One day you overhear your coworkers talking about your company, and you realize that each of them has a different idea about what their role in the company is.

Try This

As your company's emissary, you need to understand how your role relates to your company's mission and vision. You decide to write a mission statement, but you do not know how to do it. Begin by writing down how your work contributes to your company mission. Think about the values you wish to exemplify. Now put it into the context of a mission statement.

> My mission is to do my best to be our customer's provider of choice for ____; to demonstrate my care and concern for our customers by focusing on their needs; to satisfy my customers on the first try; to look for new and innovative ways to improve the products we offer; and to look for ways to grow personally.

Live up to your mission and values daily.

14. Write a Customer-Focused Plan

Why is having a plan important? Operating without a plan is the same as leaving for vacation without knowing where you are going. If you do not know your destination, you will never go in the right direction. Your mission statement is your destination. Your plan is the direction that gets you to that destination. Every plan should be customer focused. Think about this. Unless you are doing what is important to your customers, you may be headed in the wrong direction without even knowing it. A customer-focused plan keeps you headed in the right direction.

Performance Prompts

- When writing your plan, break down each component of your company or personal mission statement. What do you mean by *to satisfy customers on the first try?* In your plan, you may decide that it is unrealistic to say you will satisfy 100% of your customers, but you can work toward satisfying 98% of your customers. *I will strive to satisfy 98% of my customers on the first try by . . .*
- Include other specifics in your plan. How will you satisfy your customers? *By finding the best solution, by offering them the products that are right for their needs, by making sure those products are delivered within two days, by learning all I can about my job and company, by observing coworkers and providing specific feedback for improvement, and by asking my customers how our company can improve.*
- Include all items that are important to your mission in your plan.
- Detail all major work activities on which you want to concentrate.
- Establish time frames so you can monitor progress.
- If you are a leader writing a plan for your team, review the plan with everyone involved and make sure it is realistic.

- Make sure everything you include in your plan is important to your customers.

When This Happens . . .

You have a customer-focused plan in place for your team and decide to change the company that delivers your products. Contracting with a different carrier will be less expensive for your customers, but it will add two days to the delivery time. You are getting ready to rewrite your plan to detail this change when your coworker, James, mentions that a couple of his customers told him how much they appreciate the fast delivery you offer.

Try This

Before implementing changes to your plan, make sure it is what your customers want. You never asked your customers if speedy delivery or low rates mattered more. You decide to develop a short talk piece for you and your coworkers to use at the end of every contact that explains you are considering changing delivery carriers. Which do customers prefer: lower shipping charges with a four- to five-day delivery or the service you now provide? After doing this for one week you determine that your customers like things the way they are. Because you first asked your customers what is important to them, you averted a customer service disaster.

If it ain't broke, it might not need to be fixed.

15. Set Specific and Relevant Goals

Your mission statement is your destination, and your plan is your direction. Next, you need to map out the specific path that will move you in the direction of your destination. Setting goals is important. Without a detailed roadmap, you might head off in the wrong direction.

Performance Prompts

- Goals are the details that move you in the direction of your destination. What specific steps are you going to take to meet your 98% customer satisfaction rate? In your plan you wrote, *by learning all I can about my job and company.* Your goals will include the steps necessary to accomplish that.
- After you write down your goals, prioritize them.
- Set goals that will move you toward your mission.
- Break down large or long-term goals into smaller, step-by-step goals that will be more manageable.
- Get input from those who are directly responsible for helping you meet the goals.
- Review the goals with your team, and discuss strategies for achieving them.
- When you meet your goals, set new ones. Goal setting is a continuous process.
- Review your progress, and revise goals if they need to be changed.
- Help your coworkers set goals for themselves.

When This Happens ...

After creating your mission statement and writing your plan, you sit down to write goals. You are confused, though. Shouldn't your plan and mission statement be enough?

Try This

Wrong. The only way to make sure you stay on the right path is to put goals in writing.

Your mission statement says that you will satisfy customers on the first try.

Your plan says that you will strive to achieve a 98% customer satisfaction rating.

Your goals are going to map out what you will do to achieve the 98% rate.

For *by learning all I can about my job and company*, your goals might be:

- Review *Customer Service Training 101* by XX/XX/XX.
- Analyze all my areas of improvement by XX/XX/XX.
- Write a development plan that focuses on my individual areas of improvement by XX/XX/XX.
- Ask my manager for brush up training to be completed by XX/XX/XX.
- Schedule a tour of other departments to have a better understanding of my company operation by XX/XX/XX.

Do less, but do it better.

16. Measure Results to Stay on Track

Now that you know your destination, figured out the best direction to take, and mapped out your path to success, you need to devise a way to measure your achievements. That is the only way you will know whether you are staying on track. Why measure? Because it brings focus to achieving company goals, it shows how effective you are, it helps in setting new goals and monitoring trends, it identifies input for analyzing problem areas, it gives employees a sense of accomplishment, and it helps you monitor progress. Measurements can either be objective or subjective.

Performance Prompts

Examples of objective measurements (concrete results from actual figures):

- Customer service results (you will learn more about how to measure customer service through the customer response surveys in Chapter 7).
- Sales figures
- Revenue protection
- Accuracy
- Productivity
- Expenses
- Attendance

Examples of subjective measurements (derived from observation and opinion):

- Customer satisfaction results (you will learn more about how to monitor and measure subjective customer service in Chapter 9).
- Setting a positive example for others
- Interpersonal relations—ability to work well with others
- Adherence to established policies and procedures
- Oral and written communication
- Career development

When This Happens . . .

You have a system in place to measure customer service based on the length of time it takes to complete a customer's request. That should be good enough. After all, you do not get too many complaints from customers.

Try This

Do you measure your customer service based on what *you think your customers want?* Or do you measure your customer service based on what *your customers really want?* Measuring customer service based on internal measurements is a good idea, as long as you know it is in line with what your customers want. The only way to know how well you are actually performing is to ask your customers what is important to them. When you measure customer service results, it is important to measure objective results based on customer responses. It is equally important to measure subjective results from direct observations. Doing both ensures that your customers are happy and that you and your coworkers are held to high expectations.

Always make sure you do what is important to your customers.

CHAPTER 4

COMMUNICATION
Choose the Right Lines in the Script

"Talk low, talk slow, and don't say too much."

—JOHN WAYNE

As you are walking back into the theater to talk to Bob, you think about what you want to say. How you present the problems to Bob can either encourage him or make him defensive. If he becomes defensive, the conversation can turn into a disaster. You ask Bob if he has time to talk about a few things. He does, so you begin by telling him about the parking lot conversation. He folds his arms tightly across his body, and the look in his eyes tells you that he is starting to become angry. You explain that you are sharing what was said to help him before the next rehearsal. You add that you, too, have acted in plays previously and that you even directed a play once. You talk about the importance of having a mission, a plan, and goals. Wardrobe, set design, props, and blocking the stage are important elements of the production, and the cast is concerned that none of those things have been planned out. You assure Bob that you are all in this together and that everyone wants a good production. Bob relaxes as you talk and thanks you for being frank with him. He asks for suggestions for next rehearsal. You both agree that open communication is vital to the play's success. Bob has an "aha" moment about how communication relates to the entire production.

Actors communicate to the audience through spoken lines, gestures, body movements, facial expressions, and other actions. Speaking the lines properly means getting the message across the way it is meant. Enhancing the lines with nonverbal signals conveys the emotion behind the lines. If the cast speaks clearly and sends the correct signals, the audience can listen well. Miss the mark on either one, and good communication is blocked. It is the director's responsibility to show the actors how to best communicate their roles. Even though you are not the director of this play, taking responsibility to help Bob become a better director is going to help the entire cast.

At work, taking responsibility to put on a better production is going to help your entire business. Good communication is the heart and soul of strong customer and coworker relationships. Relationships develop when there is good communication—and break down when there is poor communication. Customer service stars who learn vital communication skills are better equipped to transfer those skills to others. Well-trained employees are better able to communicate with customers in any situation.

When you accept the role of being a customer service star, you are taking responsibility to be a better communicator with your customers, your manager, and your coworkers. You will also become a better communicator everywhere in your life. Become a better communicator and you will hear *Bravo!* and *Encore!*

"I believe that as much as you take, you have to give back. It's important not to focus on yourself too much."

—NICOLE KIDMAN

17. You Don't Communicate Alone

Communication always requires two people. In any organization, messages may be communicated up the chain of command, down through the ranks, across the same level, inside the company, outside the company, or through the grapevine. Communication may be formal or informal. Communication up or down the organization usually is more formal than communication with peers. Grapevine communication is often the most damaging because it can run rampant across, up, or down, and usually is based on rumors that become more elaborate as the vine grows longer.

Communication may be conducted face to face, by telephone, through e-mail, or by sending a written message. Face-to-face communication is effective because you pick up on body language cues and match your communication style to the other person's. Telephone communication is effective when you stay focused on the conversation. E-mail or other written communication is effective when you review and improve what you want to say before hitting the send key.

Performance Prompts

- No matter which form of communication you are using, remember that it always takes two to communicate.
- Communication involves a sender and a receiver of a message. Unless what is said and what is heard are the same, you are not communicating well.
- Words are an important component of communication, but so are the nonverbal messages you send along with your words. In other words, effective communication is a package deal.
- Delivery and timing are crucial to understanding. If you speak before gaining someone's full attention, your message might not be heard or understood correctly.

- No matter how well you communicate, keep in mind that the receivers of your messages are going to interpret them based on their experiences and states of mind.

When This Happens . . .

You have a project to assign to your coworker, Susan. You take it to her desk, but as you are explaining the project, you notice that she is working on a customer's order. When you tell her the deadline is tomorrow, she gives you a look that strongly conveys her unwillingness to take on the project, grabs it from you, and throws it onto a pile of work.

Try This

Before assigning any project, observe your coworker. If you see that the person is having a bad day or looks frazzled or stressed out, wait until the workload settles down before asking the coworker to assume additional work. Remember, timing is crucial to communicating effectively.

Are you only hearing what is being said?
Look and listen to what is really being communicated.

18. Stop When You See Communication Red Lights

Effective communication can trip on any number of obstacles. You need to be consciously awareness of the roadblocks in your path that hinder your ability to communicate well. When you send a message and receive either negative feedback or no feedback, ask yourself if you missed any communication red lights.

Performance Prompts

- Language can be a communication red light. You might unconsciously use technical phrases, jargon, company terms, acronyms, or slang that the receiver of your message does not understand.
- Accents can be a communication red light. How you pronounce your words can be confusing to others.
- Distractions can be a communication red light. When you are listening, your brain can process more words per minute than the speaker can verbalize, so your mind has idle time while you are listening. By allowing your thoughts to wander from the speaker, you may misinterpret a message.
- Nonverbal signals can be a communication red light. You can say one thing but send a completely different message.
- A person's appearance can be a communication red light. When someone is dressed inappropriately for the work situation, the listener focuses more on the person's appearance than on what the person is communicating.
- A person's attitude can be a communication red light. Present a poor attitude, and communication is blocked. You are going to focus on the attitude and not on what the person has to say.

When This Happens . . .

A customer is talking to you in a heavy accent. Although you are listening carefully, you are not sure you understand the message. You do not want to offend the person, yet you do not want to misinterpret the message and give an incorrect answer.

Try This

Do not let the customer continue without clearing up your confusion. Wait for a break and say, "I'm sorry. I'm not sure that I'm understanding you correctly. Did you say . . . ?" Saying this in a caring manner lets the customer know you are truly interested in what is being said. Continue to paraphrase what the customer says to stay on track. "OK, you would like to order____, right?"

Always match your language style to the person with whom you are communicating.

19. Go with Green Light Communication

Just as obstacles can block your path to good communication, green lights open the way for you to have an effective two-way dialogue. Focusing on the causes for communication red lights is an important first step in changing those red lights to green.

Performance Prompts

- Think before you speak and choose your words carefully. When you have a choice, choose a simple word over a complicated one.
- Be aware of your own accent, and try to speak clearly. Be aware of how you speak to people with different accents to make sure your message is clearly understood.
- Pay attention to the speaker. Try not to allow your mind to wander. Maintaining interest in the other person signals that you are listening to the message. Remember that you are going to get the ball tossed back to you. When that happens, you will want the other person to pay attention to you.
- Be aware of the nonverbal signals the other person sends along with the spoken message. Watch to see if the nonverbals match the verbals; nonverbal messages are usually the most accurate because they communicate the emotional state of the person.
- Make sure that your appearance matches the style of your workplace and your customers. Because customers see you first and hear you second, dress appropriately, and check to make sure you are well-groomed when you come in to work. Look in a full-length mirror before leaving home.
- Remember that attitude is everything—good or bad. Your attitude is what your customers will remember about your business.

When This Happens …

You are having a terrible week. Meetings, conference calls, numerous e-mail messages stacking up, calls from unhappy customers, projects and reports due. You find you are easily distracted when people talk to you.

Try This

Your customers and coworkers always deserve your full attention. Think about this: people often emulate the behavior of those around them. If you are distracted when people speak to you, do not be surprised if they treat you the same way. Send a communication green light by paying full attention when you are with others, especially your customers. And when you plan each day, schedule a block of time to spend with your coworkers. Even if you can only schedule fifteen minutes during busy days, you will feel better because you are devoting time to communicating with those around you. If you have a day when you absolutely cannot fit it into your schedule, try spending lunch or break time with your coworkers.

The best way for you to communicate with your coworkers is to spend time with them.

20. Listen, Listen, Listen

Listening is the most important part of effective communication. Listening well is more important than speaking well. Without the ability to truly listen, communication can never be effective.

Performance Prompts

- Pay close attention to the speaker. Look at the person and focus on what is being said. Tune out distractions, such as other conversations and other people.
- Listen with your entire brain. Do not allow your thoughts to wander.
- Never interrupt the speaker. Interrupting shows that you care more about what you are thinking than what the other person is saying. Only interrupt to clear up confusion or when the speaker gets off track.
- Ask questions to show you are following the speaker. *What happened when . . . ?* Using questions beginning with who, what, how, and why keeps the person talking so you can gain complete understanding.
- When the speaker is finished, show you understand by rephrasing the speaker's main points in your own words.
- Keep your emotions in check. Do not let emotional words or topics cause you to react negatively or inappropriately.
- Remain objective and avoid judging the speaker. Never jump to conclusions before hearing the entire message.
- Are you only hearing what is being said? Listen for what is really being communicated.
- While you are listening, pay attention to the speaker's nonverbal communication to make sure the words match the body language.

When This Happens . . .

You are listening to a customer tell you about a problem he had on a previous call to your company. He is upset and is starting to ramble and get off track. You are afraid you are going to miss the message and not understand what the actual problem is. You do not want to interrupt him, though, while he is speaking.

Try This

This is a time when a polite interruption is appropriate. Wait for a lull, then interject, "I'm sorry that happened, and I'm going to help resolve this for you. When you told the employee you wouldn't be home yesterday and needed a different appointment date, what did the employee say to you?" This will guide the customer back on track.

The more you talk, the less you listen.

21. Speak Your Best at All Times

When you are speaking, you are in control of the conversation—as long as you are saying something to which the listener is receptive. Delivery is an important part of speaking. How you say something—that is, the tone and timing of your message—is just as important as the words you choose.

Performance Prompts

- Be clear and precise. Think about what you want to say before you open your mouth.
- Speak effectively by stating exactly what you mean in a positive and assertive manner.
- Be specific. Focus on communicating one idea at a time.
- Make eye contact when you speak. Eye contact communicates confidence and honesty.
- When speaking to new people, keep your emotions out of the conversation.
- Assess your audience, and speak to their level of understanding.
- Assess the situation before launching into a conversation. Now might not be a good time.
- Make it a habit to never use profanity, jargon, slang, or clichés.
- Return phone calls promptly. Be dependable.
- When making a call, identify your company and your name before jumping into your conversation.
- Erase the words *I can't* from your vocabulary. Instead, stress what you *can* do.
- When speaking to others, choose words and a tone that do not patronize listeners.
- Vary your tone, pitch, and loudness. People are more likely to stay with a speaker whose voice is interesting to listen to.

When This Happens . . .

You need to speak to a manager about a problem you had with one of her employees. As you walk into her cubicle, she is working on a project. She barely looks up as she mumbles, "Hi." You begin explaining the problem you had with the way Ken handled a customer. Now, the customer is upset and wants a refund. She looks at you and says, "I don't have time for this. Just deal with it." This is not how you thought the conversation would go. This is not the first time Ken caused a customer problem, and you do not want to just deal with it.

Try This

This is clearly not the right time to talk to the manager about an employee problem. When you first saw that she was working on a project, you might have asked, "Is this a good time for us to talk?" That would have shown that you are considerate. Her answer will tell you if she is receptive. If not, schedule a time to get together.

Be a considerate communicator by learning good timing.

22. Pay Attention to Body Language: Yours and Others

Tone and body language account for a major part of communication. Feelings and emotions are reflected outward and picked up through certain expressions, gestures, and even posture. You can learn a lot about people through nonverbal communication.

Performance Prompts

- Smile. A smile communicates into any language and culture. Smile warmly, and smile as often as appropriate.
- Your face can be a snapshot of your attitude and emotions. Make sure your facial expressions match what you are saying. When listening, smile, look excited, show concern, or remain passive. Match your facial expressions to the conversation.
- Make eye contact when communicating, but not to the point where you appear to be staring or glaring. Because a person's eyes are thought to be the windows to the soul, pay attention to the other person's eyes to pick up on nonverbal cues.
- Show your interest by keeping your attention on the speaker. Try not to interrupt but if you must, wait until an interruption is appropriate.
- Maintain a relaxed and open demeanor through good posture and by keeping your hands naturally at your sides unless you are gesturing to emphasize what you are saying.
- Gestures should flow naturally. If they are too exaggerated, people will pay more attention to your movements than to what you are saying.

Here are some signals to watch for in others.

- Exaggerated gestures may signal overexcitement—or anger.
- Failure to make eye contact may mean shyness—or dishonesty or distraction.

- Fidgeting may be a sign of nervousness—or agitation.
- Smiling more often or more broadly than normal may signal happiness—or lying.
- Arms folded across the body may mean the person is cold—or threatened or close minded.
- A higher than normal pitch may be a sign of excitement—or nervousness.

When This Happens …

A customer confronts you about a problem she had with one of your coworkers. You are scheduled to give a presentation to your manager in less than an hour, and you find yourself fidgeting and looking at the notes on your desk rather than at your customer. You catch yourself sending negative nonverbal signals and thinking, *now is not a good time for this.*

Try This

Remember customers are number one. If you stay focused, you will be able to help the customer more quickly. Stop fidgeting, make eye contact, listen carefully, show concern, and nod from time to time. Now you are sending the message that she is important to you. Tune in so you can find the best solution efficiently and effectively.

Actions always speak louder than words.

23. Give and Get Accurate Information

The importance of giving and getting accurate information cannot be understated. If you and the person with whom you are communicating get it right the first time, you will not need a second time. Staying focused, paying attention, speaking clearly, and answering any questions will enhance your communication skills.

Performance Prompts

- Never assume. You know what happens when you assume.
- Make sure it is a good time for the conversation.
- Keep your emotions in check if the conversation is heating up.
- You cannot be open-minded if you are not objective.

Giving accurate information:

- Write down the key points you want to say or ask.
- Check for accuracy before sharing information with others.
- If necessary, ask a coworker to review your information for accuracy.
- Explain why you are asking or why you are giving information to help the other person be more receptive.
- Use open-ended questions to get adequate answers.

Receiving accurate information:

- Hear the person out so you do not jump to conclusions.
- If you are not sure what the other person is looking for, say so.
- Ask follow-up questions to make sure you understood correctly.
- Recap before responding.

When This Happens …

You need to explain to your coworkers about a new company policy that is going to affect some work shifts. This is not going to sit well with them. You want to make sure they stay tuned in as this policy will affect their jobs and, maybe, their attitudes.

Try This

First help your coworkers understand *why* you are asking them to make this change. Do not make light of what you are saying. Rather, keep an objective point of view. They might not agree, but if they understand the reason for the change, you are more likely to gain their acceptance. For example, say something like, "We've discovered a scheduling problem for our customers. To accommodate their needs, we're going to schedule our deliveries to begin at a later time each day. That's going to mean rescheduling some shifts, and while I realize this may create problems for those of you who will have to work later, we need to do this to keep our customers satisfied. Let me tell you about it, and then we'll discuss how we can best meet everyone's needs." Now state specifically what the change is. Ask questions to ensure understanding, and listen closely to the responses.

Allowing others to share in some decisions
will make it easier for them to accept
the decisions you are not able to let them share.

24. Ask Good Questions

We ask questions for a variety of reasons. At work, we mainly ask questions to gain a better understanding of a situation. Questions make up a large part of business communication. Learning to ask better and more focused questions enhances your communication skills, whether you are engaged in a business conversation or a conversation with your friends at a social gathering.

Performance Prompts

- If you have an idea of what type information you are going to need, prepare some questions in advance.
- Move on to the next question only after you are sure you have answered the previous question adequately.
- Look at the situation from more than one viewpoint, and always try to keep an open mind when you ask questions.
- Formulate your questions so that you do not sound like an interrogator.
- When you are done asking questions, summarize your understanding of the answers.

Here are some techniques that will help you be a better questioner:

- Before launching into a series of questions, first make sure your timing is good.
    - *In order to help you, I'm going to need to ask you some questions. Is that OK?*
    - *Can we talk this over? If I have more information, I think I'll have a better understanding of why this happened.*
- If you want to understand feelings and emotions, encourage the person to talk.
    - *Tell me about that.*
    - *How did you feel when . . . ?*

- If you need additional information, ask for it.
    - *I'd like more information about that.*
    - *What else do you think you'll need?*
- If you are confused, ask the person to clarify or give you more information.
    - *I don't understand. Can you explain it to me?*
    - *Can you give me an example?*

When This Happens . . .

This afternoon you are meeting with an important client about some new computer programs your company developed. She is interested in upgrading her system.

Try This

Before your meeting, formulate questions to help you gain information that will enhance your proposal. Begin by asking, "Would it be all right if I ask you a few questions? I'd like to have a better understanding of your needs so I can determine which of our new computer programs might be good for you." Next, ask questions that encourage an emotional response. "What happens when . . . ?" is a good starting point to get specific information that will make your proposal more effective.

Ask good questions and you will get good answers.

25. Ask Who, What, When, Where, Why, and How

Questions may either be closed or open. Closed questions require a yes, no, or short answer. They are effective in controlling the conversation. When you need short answers to clarify information or when you need a specific yes or no, use questions beginning with *is, are, do, can,* or *will.* Open questions, on the other hand, require longer answers. When you need information or want to get someone talking, use open questions beginning with *who, what, when, where, why,* and *how.*

Performance Prompts

- To encourage thoughts or feelings, try:
  - *Who, in your opinion, would like to . . . ?*
  - *What do you think about . . . ?*
  - *Why is it important that . . . ?*
- To gather additional information, try:
  - *When do you . . . ?*
  - *Where would you . . . ?*
  - *How do you . . . ?*
- To clarify information, try:
  - *Is one going to be . . . ?*
  - *Are you going to use it to . . . ?*
  - *Do you . . . ?*
  - *Can you . . . ?*
  - *Will you . . . ?*
- To guide the other person to make a decision, try:
  - *What you are saying is . . . , right?*
  - *Let's recap what we've discussed. . . . Is that correct?*
  - *I want to make sure I understand correctly. . . . Am I on target?*
  - *You said that you. . . . Will this help?*

When This Happens . . .

You are helping your customer reach a decision about your proposal. When you are in the questioning mode, let the other person do most of the talking so you can listen closely to uncover her needs.

Try This

Use open questions to keep the person talking, then switch to closed questions to reach a conclusion. Ask the open question, "What happens when . . . ?" When you recap, turn the customer's answer into a closed question, "You mentioned that when . . . , _____ happens, right? Our product can solve that problem by. . . ." You painted a picture in the customer's mind by using a problem the customer is having to propose your solution. By adding *right?* at the end of the sentence you are gaining the customer's agreement.

Be careful when beginning a question with "why" that you don't put the person on the defensive.

26. Respond to Enhance Communication

How you respond to others can foster open communication or it can smother it. If a coworker is excitedly telling you about an idea and you answer in a bored or distracted manner, what type of message are you sending to your coworker? Pay attention to the way you respond, and focus on answering in a positive way.

Performance Prompts

- Nodding while someone is speaking lets the person know you are interested.
- Matching your facial expressions to the person's speech lets the person know you are on the same page.
- Try to match your answer to the person's mood. When someone is sad, use a caring and considerate tone in your response. When someone is excited, smile and show that you appreciate the enthusiasm.
- Giving a positive response encourages the other person to talk.
- If you have to disagree, focus on the issue, not the person, and explain your feelings on the situation.
- Try to control your use of *but.* When someone hears *that's a great idea, but . . . ,* it is an instant downer. You can still get your point across *and* eliminate the *buts. That's a great idea, and I wish we could implement it.*
- Use *I* rather than *You* when responding to something that upsets you. *I'm upset that I got the report late again,* sounds better than, *You always turn your reports in late. I* puts the focus on how *I* feel about the situation. Focusing on *you* will likely make the other person defensive.
- Rarely are things *always* or *never.* You might be tempted to use these words for emphasis when you are upset. Don't.

- If the other person is emotional, reflect his feelings. *It sounds like that really made you angry.* The other person knows you care and are tuned in.

When This Happens . . .

Your coworker, Chris, is telling you that her last customer was upset by what she said. After relating the story, she ends by saying how ridiculous the customer was. She is looking for you to take her side, but you see the situation from a different perspective.

Try This

Nod while she is talking to show you are listening closely. When she finishes, start your conversation by stating how you feel. "From a customer perspective, if someone said that to me, I would have been upset because it sounded as though I was at fault. Next time this type of situation comes up, try saying it like this. . . . I think you'll find customers will be more receptive hearing it that way."

> *Show you value the other person by always giving more than a one word answer when answering or responding.*

27. Assure to Make Others Feel Valued

Assuring means instilling positive feelings in another person. At work, you have many occasions to assure people. In co-worker situations, you assure to instill confidence, to open up communication, and to help people overcome insecurities. In customer situations, you assure about buying decisions and when customers are hesitant about committing to a proposed solution.

Performance Prompts

- Putting yourself in another person's shoes helps you empathize. It is easier to assure others if you can see the situation from their perspective.
- When you see the situation from someone else's perspective, you will be able to offer the best solution to that person.
- Always offer what is right for the other person, not what you think is right.
- Validate the person's decision. Even if you do not agree with the decision, help the other person save face. *I understand how you feel.*
- Instill positive feelings, and never make someone feel bad about a decision. *You need to do what's right for you. I respect that.*
- If you cannot think of an appropriate response to someone who is obviously making the wrong decision, it is all right to say, *Let me think about that, and I'll get back to you so we can discuss it further.* This buys you time to come up with a good response.

When This Happens . . .

You spent an hour explaining the benefits of one of your new computer programs to your customer. You are certain this program is going to benefit her company by saving time and money. When she says, "I don't know. Let me think about it, and I'll get back to you," you are disappointed.

Try This

You want to assure the customer, and you would also like her to commit to a decision now. You can assure her *and* help her reach a decision. Try one of these statements. Assure her by saying, "I can understand this is a big decision for you.

Next, help her reach a decision by asking another question.

What other questions do you have?"
What are your thoughts about this product?"
What is it that you aren't sure about?"
What are you hesitant about?"

The best way to assure others is to always make them feel valued and respected.

28. Zap Zapper Words from Your Vocabulary

You have heard them. You have most likely said them. Those words—usually small, seemingly insignificant words—that zap the energy right out of you. Those words that kill a person's ambition, creativity, or even hope. Read the list below, very carefully, and make sure you rid your vocabulary of these zapper words and phrases.

Performance Prompts

Try to never ever say:

- No.
- I can't.
- That won't work.
- It's too hard.
- We could never do that.
- We've tried that before.
- I don't have time.
- I'm too busy.
- We better not.
- You don't understand.
- You can't do that.
- We don't want to change things.
- Sounds good, but. . . .

When This Happens . . .

You listened to a presentation by your coworker, Ray, about a new product he developed. You like his idea, but you are going to have to say no. Think how Ray is going to feel if you say, "It's a good idea, but no, we couldn't possibly do that. We're keeping things the way they are and can't implement any new products right now." It sounds as though you are blowing Ray off and that you do not value the time he spent developing his idea. Answering this way is likely to squash Ray's creativity.

Try This

How can you say no without saying no? It is not hard to do. You can respond to Ray and help him feel good at the same time. It is all in the wording you choose. Try something like this. "Wow, Ray, I can tell you put a lot of time and energy into your idea, and I appreciate your creativity. I'm impressed that you developed this product, and I'd like you to share your idea at our next staff meeting. Even though our owner just made the decision to keep our existing product line for the next three months, when we can add new products everyone will be familiar with what you developed." You said no without using the *no* word. You omitted the *but* word. You empathized with Ray and assured him. You helped him feel good about his idea.

Helping others save face is a valuable quality.

29. Charge Ahead with Charger Words

Zapper words rob us of our strength and energy, while charger words lift us up, energize us, ignite a fire in us, build confidence, and invigorate our self-esteem. Erase all zappers, and replace them with the following energizers.

Performance Prompts

Try to say one, some, or all of these everyday:

- Yes.
- I can.
- You can.
- That's great.
- Let's try it.
- I like it.
- Sounds good.
- I agree.
- Great job.
- I'm glad you thought of that.
- I appreciate your effort.
- I know you can do it.
- Good for you.
- I never would have thought of that.
- I'm happy for you.

More words to use more often:

- Will you? (rather than You will).
- You could. (rather than You should.)
- How can I help?
- Thank you.
- I'm sorry.
- I made a mistake.
- What can I do to correct this?

When This Happens …

You are speaking with a customer who is upset with your company. He sat home all morning waiting for a delivery that did not arrive. There is no way for you to undo what already happened. What you say next can either calm the customer or upset him further.

Try This

"Mr. Johnson, I'm sorry we made that mistake. Let me check right now to see what I can do for you." Your confidence and positive and assertive reply will show Mr. Johnson that you care and want to get this resolved.

Always focus on what you can do rather than on what you can't do.

CHAPTER 5

LEADERSHIP
Great Performances Need Great Direction

"It takes tremendous discipline to control the influence, the power you have over other people's lives."

—CLINT EASTWOOD

Today is your second rehearsal. You have not spoken to Bob since your conversation following your last rehearsal about the problems, so you are a little on edge. He begins the rehearsal by saying, "I thought the first rehearsal went okay until afterward when one of you talked to me about some problems." He makes a face that breaks the ice, and the cast laughs. "Seriously, though, I am new at directing, and I've thought a lot about my responsibilities. I'm confident that today's rehearsal will go better. You may remember that when we were together for the auditions, one of the producers said some things after you were cast. He said that there are no minor roles in this play; that every role is important; that each character makes up the cast; and it is the cast who puts on the production. Every one of us must work together to make this production great. If one person doesn't play a part well, the play can flop. At our first rehearsal, I didn't play my part very well and I apologize for that. Going forward let's remember that we are all in this together. Just as you look to me to help you improve, I'm going to look to you to help me improve." Bob winks at you. He got it!

Bob got it because you took a leadership role and talked to him about the problems. Would he have gotten it if you hadn't? Most likely, he would have assumed he was doing everything he was supposed to do. As you walk to your car after rehearsal, the parking lot conversation is quite different. The cast is pumped up and everyone agrees that today's rehearsal was productive. Bob demonstrated leadership skills by listening, giving specific feedback, and encouraging everyone to work together, so that all of you are equipped to put on a great production.

When you walk into work every day and get into your customer service role, no matter what part you were chosen to play, play it well. You are all in this production together; do your best to make it great. Every performance begins with great leadership, and great leadership does not always come from the top. Leaders are found at every level, and they are found in every role in life. When you become a leader at work, you become a star at work.

Remember that every actor is a director, and every director is an actor. Each frontline employee is a manager, and each manager is a frontline employee. Each person in your organization can rise to stardom by developing leadership qualities.

You may wonder what leadership has to do with customer service. The answer is more than you think. Leaders take responsibility to give exceptional customer service. Leaders also take responsibility to improve themselves, their team, and their company to make things better for their customers. Leaders use critical-thinking skills to make sound decisions. They manage their time well to increase output. Most importantly, customer service leaders add value to everything they do.

"All through my career I've done what I can to discover new talent and give them a start."

—STEVEN SPIELBERG

30. Positive Leadership Begins with Awareness

Look around. Who are the leaders in your organization? Your first inclination may be to think of people in upper management or ownership positions as the leaders in your company, but look closely. You will find leaders at every level. Although there are born leaders, positive leadership consists of qualities you can develop. If you want to become a leader, start by developing an awareness of the qualities that set positive leaders apart from others. Study leaders you respect. Read about historical leaders who have had a positive impact on their world. What qualities did they possess that made them effective leaders?

Think about this: all leaders are not positive leaders. Some leaders are dictators, who centralize authority within themselves and control others. Some leaders are permissive, avoid power, and allow others to set goals, solve problems, and make decisions. And some leaders are participative leaders, who strike the right balance between centralizing authority and sharing authority. Participative leadership is motivational leadership.

Performance Prompts

Participative leaders are powerful, positive leaders. They:

- Strive to live up to the corporate mission and values.
- Have a vision for the future.
- Inspire others to follow their vision.
- Set goals for self-development.
- Trust their instincts and abilities.
- Are not afraid to take risks or make mistakes.
- Take responsibility for mistakes.
- Understand that knowledge is power.
- Look for opportunities to continually grow and improve.
- Want those around them to be the best they can be.

- Share information and power.
- Share success with others, but take personal responsibility for failure.
- Foster teamwork by building trust.
- Are not afraid of challenge.
- Develop the flexibility to roll with the punches.
- Develop the ability to adapt quickly to change.

When This Happens . . .

You admire your coworker, Caroline, because she exemplifies leadership qualities. You wish you could be like her, but you do not think that is possible because you are quiet and shy.

Try This

Being aware of the qualities that set Caroline apart from other employees is your first step to developing leadership qualities. Tell yourself that you can become a leader like Caroline and think about the leadership qualities you wish to develop.

Take responsibility for you.

31. Develop Positive Leadership Qualities

Now that you are becoming aware of the qualities leaders possess, you have the first draft of your script for self-development. Read the script carefully. You may already possess some of these qualities. You may need to strengthen others. And some you may need to learn completely.

Performance Prompts

- Make a list of the leadership traits you wish to develop. Customer service leaders strive to become ethical, honest, trustful, competent, flexible, goal oriented, energetic, self-confident, loyal, good communicators, and inspirations to others.
- Self-assess your leadership qualities as you see yourself today.
- Make a list of your strengths, areas of improvement, and weaknesses.
- Set goals for each area of improvement and weakness.
- When setting goals, be realistic about your development. For major weaknesses (such as the need to overcome shyness), set step-by-step goals. Start small, but think big.
- As you work toward each goal, think of consistency. To master each of the leadership qualities, you must consistently display the desired behaviors.
- When you reach your goals by consistently displaying the goal behavior, move the quality to your list of strengths.
- Read your list daily as a reminder of the leadership role you are learning and rehearsing.

When This Happens . . .

You identified being a good communicator as one of your areas of improvement. For you, this means becoming more outgoing. Occasionally, you move outside of your comfort zone by forcing yourself to be outgoing, but by nature you are quiet and reserved. How do you set goals to change?

Try This

The fact that you occasionally are able to force yourself out of your comfort zone means you have already taken the first step toward changing your behavior. Understanding who you are and who you want to be means you are on the right track to becoming a better communicator. Set a goal to be outgoing and friendly every day. If that seems too daunting, break that goal into smaller, easier-to-reach goals. Your first goal could be to start a conversation with one new person every day. As you become more comfortable, being outgoing will become second nature. Soon your shyness will be a thing of the past and you will find yourself becoming more comfortable when communicating.

Don't wait for others to set goals for you.
Start setting them for yourself.

32. Think Like a Leader

You identified the traits you want to develop. You set goals to change your behavior. Now it is time to practice, practice, practice. The only way for you to become a leader is to think like a leader. Envision yourself already possessing the leadership qualities you are developing. Visualize yourself already being a leader.

Performance Prompts

Think like a leader by:

- Preparing for the role of participative and positive leader through visualization.
- Envisioning yourself projecting leadership behaviors.
- Rehearsing continually and practicing your leadership role every day.
- Focusing on your positive qualities.
- Turning negative self-talk into positive affirmations.
- Affirming daily that you are a leader.
- Listening carefully to positive self-talk and affirmations.
- Seeking challenging opportunities.
- Continually looking for ways to improve.
- Always asking yourself, *What would a leader do in this situation?*

When This Happens . . .

One of your self-development goals is to take more risks. You want to volunteer to take on a major project, but you are leery about taking risks. Perhaps you will not know how to manage a project while you are still developing your leadership skills. Maybe you should wait until you feel more comfortable.

Try This

Why wait? Think like a leader. Change your self-talk to *I am ready for this. As a leader, I will take responsibility to do a great job.*

Talk to your manager, and explain that part of your personal development plan is taking on a major project, something you have not done before. Assure your manager that you are willing to take full responsibility to do a great job, and do your best. Ask your manager to assign you a project. Enlist the help of a trusted peer, such as Caroline, to be available if you have any problems. Seek out a mentor who will work with you and provide you with feedback as you develop your leadership qualities.

Always take personal responsibility.
This is what will set you apart.

33. Model Leadership Behavior

Once you begin thinking like a leader, the next step is to shine in your leadership role. You set goals and practiced. You envisioned yourself displaying leadership qualities. Now it is time for you to *be* a leader. Every day, in everything you do, do it as a leader.

Performance Prompts

- Leadership is an active process. You must constantly see yourself as a leader, think like a leader, and project leadership behavior.
- Every day make a good impression by dressing for success, smiling often, listening well, communicating clearly, staying interested in others, and treating everyone with respect.
- It is easier to lead when you believe in your vision and mission.
- You set the example. Set it well.
- Work hard to earn people's trust, and then work harder to keep it.
- People will follow your lead if they trust you enough to stand behind you. Build trust by showing others that you will stand behind them.
- People would rather be around those who are positive. Always display positive leadership qualities.
- People want to be around those who are enthusiastic. Maintain a high energy level throughout the day to maintain a can-do attitude.
- Be consistent with your team and coworkers. People want to know they can expect the same treatment from you day to day.
- Never act as though you are above doing any job. Lead the way through those tasks everyone dislikes.
- Every day do something to help someone.

When This Happens …

At lunch today your coworker, Brandon, made a sarcastic remark about your boss to your lunch group. Everyone, but you, is laughing and making jokes. He notices that you are not joining in and says, "What's happening to you? You've changed a lot. You're no fun anymore."

Try This

Let's face it. You are changing. People are going to notice. Some people, like Brandon, may even feel threatened. Be proud of your changes. When your coworkers make snide comments about your new persona, try one of these comebacks.

- "You're right, I have made some changes. I decided that I can go through life being negative and looking for things to complain about, or I can go through life trying to make a positive impact on others. I like myself better this way."
- "Making the decision to stop being negative and talking about people *has* changed me, and I'm happy with the change. I'm not going there anymore."
- "Thanks for noticing the changes. I'm focusing on being the best person I can be."

Treat everyone as though they are equally important to you.

34. Learn Critical Thinking Skills

Critical thinking is an important skill to develop. Critical thinkers consider problems carefully before making decisions. Critical thinking is reflective thought about issues and situations that have no clear-cut answers or solutions.

Performance Prompts

Develop the following skills to become a critical thinker:

- Focus on the question or problem.
- Ask questions to clarify the situation or issue.
- Analyze all arguments or proposed solutions.
- Ask yourself how reliable or credible is your source of information.
- Make value judgments about all possible solutions.
- Keep an open mind. Be objective.
- Decide on the best action.
- Communicate your decision effectively.
- Show sensitivity to other people's feelings.

When you develop these critical thinking skills, you will:

- Only involve yourself in what is necessary and what is positive.
- Not allow yourself to become involved in the negative trappings of the grapevine.
- Never assume responsibility for someone else's problems.
- Stop worrying about the things over which you have no control.
- Understand the difference between useful information and idle gossip.

When This Happens . . .

Andrew, your manager, is late to a meeting and rushes to your desk. "I need your help. Mike just stormed into my office complaining about the new ordering system that goes into effect tomorrow. He says no one understands what they're supposed to do. Make sure you retrain everyone right away so we're on board for tomorrow, OK?"

Try This

On face value, it sounds as though this is a big problem. You assure Andrew by saying, "I'll take care of it." Now kick into your critical thinking mode. Focus on the problem. You were in the same training class and fully understand the new procedures. You need to ask some questions to clarify and analyze the situation. First, explain to Mike that Andrew asked you to take care of the problem, and ask him what is going on. You know Mike to be a person who flies off the handle easily and may not be a credible source. As you listen to him, you realize that overall he knows what to do but does not understand one aspect of the new procedure. Next, individually ask the other members of the group about their understanding. As you assess the information, you realize that some of your coworkers understand the new procedures just fine, while others have questions on the same step Mike does not understand. Putting your critical thinking skills to work enables you to reach your own conclusion about the problem.

Establish a reputation as a person of good judgment.

35. Make Solid Decisions

Every day you make decisions. Some decisions are easy to make. *What should I have for breakfast? What time should I leave for work?* Some decisions require instant resolution. *What should I do when the fire alarm sounds? What alternate route can I take when I see road construction ahead?* Some decisions require research and review before reaching a conclusion. *What is the best approach to retraining my coworkers? Should I place a bid on a larger home or remodel my current home?* Developing sound resolution skills requires critical thinking and thoughtful analysis to make solid, rather than impetuous, decisions.

Performance Prompts

When making individual decisions:

- Use your critical thinking skills and analyze all information before considering a possible solution.
- Gather as much information from as many sources as you feel are necessary before you evaluate possible solutions.
- Never jump to conclusions before hearing all sides.
- Before making any decision, analyze all aspects of the situation.
- Consider all possibilities and alternatives before finalizing decisions.
- Consider the impact of your proposed solution.
- Select the best solution based on available research and information.

When making group decision:

- Discuss the situation with the group.
- Involve coworkers by describing the problem and telling them specifically how they will be participating in the decision.

- Allow all members to voice opinions and clarify ideas before reaching a decision.
- When possible, strive to reach decisions through consensus among all members.
- If you must make the decision for the group, explain the problem, why you are making the decision for the group, how you reached your decision, and what the decision is.

When This Happens . . .

Andrew suggested that you retrain everyone. After putting your critical thinking skills into action by researching and analyzing the problem, however, you realize that the solution is much simpler.

Try This

You are the one making the decision on this. There is no need to involve the members of your team. So, after reaching your decision, explain that you analyzed what needs to be done before tomorrow and that you will be retraining anyone who has questions. When Andrew returns from his meeting, give him a heads up and continue spot training, making sure everyone is comfortable with the new procedures.

Don't wait for someone else to make decisions for you.

36. Manage Your Time or Your Time Will Manage You

What does time management have to do with leadership and giving great customer service? A lot, actually. When you are organized you feel more in control, more confident, and more calm. When you feel this way, you will work more efficiently and effectively.

Performance Prompts

- Use "to do" lists daily. Prioritize each item.
- Plan only about three-quarters of your day, allowing time for the unexpected.
- When making your daily plan, schedule a block of time at the end of the day to review and plan for the next day.
- Prepare step-by-step plans for each project by breaking it down into smaller steps and scheduling the time necessary to complete each step.
- Take control of your time—if you do not, other people will.
- When you call someone who is a talker, start your conversation with *I'm really busy right now but I need to ask you about* _____. This sets the tone for the conversation.
- If someone asks for help when you are busy say. *I'll be happy to help you but now is not a good time. Let's schedule a time that will be good.*
- When spending time on hold on the telephone, read your e-mail or work through a folder of miscellaneous tasks.
- Organize your desk and keep your workspace uncluttered.
- Delegate work whenever possible.
- Learn to say no.
- When people come to you with a problem, ask for their proposed solution.
- Stop procrastinating. Make your attitude, *I'll get it done now,* rather than, *I'll do it later.*

When This Happens . . .

Barry called with a question and wants to continue talking after your business conversation ends. You have a ton of work on your desk, and you have commitments to call customers.

Try This

Take control of the conversation by saying, "I'd love to talk but I have customer commitments I need to meet."

Other examples for wanting to end a conversation are:

"I'd love to talk but. . . .

- . . . I have a report due in fifteen minutes."
- . . . I have to prepare for a meeting."
- . . . I have an appointment and I'm running late."
- . . . I've got a lot of work to get done."

The bottom line is to learn to stay in control.

We all have the same amount of time in a day—
it's what we do with it that is important.

37. Add Value to Everything You Do

Remember there is only one person who controls your performance—and that person is You. You decide how well you perform. Be someone who adds value to your organization, as well as to everything you do. You will feel good about yourself when you know you have given your all.

Performance Prompts

- Give each day 110%.
- Learn your job well.
- Ask questions to learn more.
- Do not expect your manager to be aware of everything. Initiate discussions about problem areas.
- Be accountable for your actions.
- When you make a mistake, tell your boss about it.
- Keep up to date on workplace changes.
- Learn to be flexible and adaptable.
- Step up to the plate, and volunteer for nonpopular projects.
- If you have an idea for improvement, discuss it with your manager.
- Never complain about your boss, a coworker, or your company. If you have a problem, talk to the responsible person about it.
- Think of your place of employment as your own company. Think of yourself as the owner of your company when making decisions.
- Try to come up with better ways to do things.
- Appreciate the job you have. It will show in your work.
- Contribute more than you cost.
- Add enough value that you are missed when you are not at work.

When This Happens . . .

You spent two hours creating a spreadsheet only to find out that you input last year's figures instead of this year's. Now you have to start from scratch. Most likely, only your coworker Brad, who heard you grumbling, will know. It is your call whether to tell your manager, Jennifer, about it or just start over.

Try This

If you do not talk to Jennifer, she may wonder why it is taking you so long to complete the spreadsheet. Brad may inadvertently say something. You risk losing her trust and confidence if you do not deal with this in a straightforward way. Do what is right, and talk to her. "Jennifer, I just realized I made a huge mistake on the spreadsheet. I input last year's data and didn't catch the mistake until I was almost done. I'm really sorry. I spent two hours on this, and I'm going to have to start over. I'll stay as long as it takes to input the data, and I'll have the complete report on your desk first thing tomorrow morning." You made a mistake, yet you added value by taking responsibility for your actions and making things right. Jennifer will appreciate your honesty and accountability.

Being good at what you do makes doing it a pleasure.

CHAPTER 6

PREPARATION

Things Are Going to Change

"People are always telling me that change is good. But all that means is that something you didn't want to happen has happened."

—MEG RYAN

After weeks of rehearsals, you are prepared. Tomorrow is opening night, and you are anxiously excited. You are ready for your last technical rehearsal and everyone, except Ann, one of the customer service actors, is on stage. Soon you understand why. Ann hobbles into the theater—on crutches! She explains that she fell and broke her leg. With a cast up to her right knee, you quickly surmise the outcome. You look to Bob, who springs into action. "Wow, Ann, that's awful," he says. "I'm sorry that after all the weeks you spent preparing for this role you're not going to be able to perform. You're a great asset to our cast, and I know everyone will agree that the show isn't going to be the same without you." He looks around, spots Ann's understudy, Liz, and says, "Liz, you know what this means. As soon as you can get dressed, we'll begin our final rehearsal." Bob assures Ann that she will be welcomed back as soon as her leg heals. You think back to your conversation with Bob on the first night of rehearsal, and you are proud of the way he has developed his directing skills to handle this problem.

Bob and the cast are experiencing an unforeseeable change. How quickly they are able to adjust to the change depends on how prepared they are for the unexpected. Because Bob was well prepared and developed Ann's understudy, the cast will be less fearful about the outcome and more confident as they adjust to working with Liz. Can you imagine, though, how Bob would have reacted had he not prepared himself for change? What if he did not bother to have an understudy rehearse for each role? Ann's broken leg surely would have blindsided him.

In life one thing is certain: change is inevitable. Whether it is at work, at home, or in social situations, your life is going to continually change. Change may happen expectedly with anticipation and hope or unexpectedly with shock and fear, but change will happen. Change may only take an instant to occur, but it takes time to adjust to it. It is a process involving a series of stages you must work through before you can move into a new comfort zone. The better prepared you are to deal with change, the better prepared you will be to move through this process with courage and confidence.

At work, change can blindside any organization. Change can quickly deteriorate customer service, productivity, and morale. As a customer service star, it is up to you to learn about the change process, so you can help yourself and others as changes occur.

Customer service stars become quick change artists when they understand the process and help others work through the phases; are able to keep their objectivity; maintain a positive attitude; find ways to stay accountable; and continue to give exceptional customer service while working through the change process. Learn to become a quick change artist at work, and you will be able to deal with any life event in a realistic, positive, and constructive manner.

"We all have big changes in our lives
that are more or less a second chance."

—HARRISON FORD

38. Get Ready: Things Will Not Stay the Same

No matter how much you might like things to remain status quo, they will not stay that way. The truth is there is nothing you can do about change; it is simply part of living. Any change, even a change that you welcome, is going to force you out of your comfort zone. As a result, you will lose confidence. Whether you are implementing the change or life throws you a curve, the quicker you adapt and work through the change process, the quicker you will regain your confidence and move forward.

Performance Prompts

- Change is a process, not an event.
- View any change as an opportunity to grow, develop, explore, and improve.
- No matter how exciting the change, you will feel a sense of loss.
- No matter how competent you are, you will feel a sense of uncertainty.
- Expect the loss and uncertainty to undermine your self-confidence.
- People process change in various ways. Some thrive on change, some adapt easily, some struggle to accept it, and some are not going to like it no matter what. How do you process change?
- Thriving on change may not be your style, but learning to be adaptable and flexible will help you work through the process more easily.
- Take personal responsibility to move through the change process by focusing on top priorities.
- Go easy on yourself when you are moving through the change process. Focus only on those things that are necessary.

- Look ahead to the end result of the change. Look for the positives.
- When change is thrown at you, take time to adjust to what is happening. Then, move quickly into a problem solving mode.
- Bounce back with resiliency. Resilient people deal with change more effectively.

When This Happens . . .

During a meeting, your manager announces that your company has been bought out and effective two months from now you will be working for a company headquartered in Miami. You live in New Jersey! Even though he assures you that your jobs are secure, you immediately feel a sense of shock, fear, and uncertainty.

Try This

Allow yourself some time to process the news. It is normal to feel a sense of despair. After all, this is not only a major corporate change, it is a major life change. During this time, be good to yourself. Eat a healthy diet, get plenty of rest, take time to play, take time to reflect. Just remember to bounce back with resiliency. You will be better prepared when you are adaptable and flexible.

Be ready for change by looking for areas to improve.

39. Become a Quick Change Artist

We all have choices when facing change. We can embrace change as an opportunity to grow and improve, or we can fight it and become angry and bitter. Learning to become a quick-change artist does not mean that you will make light of life's tough times. It means that you face any change head-on. Being a quick-change artist means you are able to regroup and move from feeling confused and uncertain to being a problem solver who finds new opportunities in change.

Performance Prompts

- Become a quick change artist by being flexible, adaptable, resilient, and unafraid.
- Lead rather than follow the change process.
- Show others the way by displaying quick change-artist characteristics.
- Look for new opportunities when change comes.
- Take responsibility for the change process.
- Focus on the end result.
- Keep your sense of humor.
- Keep an objective perspective.
- Be supportive of those around you: your customers, your coworkers, and management.
- Go easy on yourself when moving through change.
- When change happens, use your critical-thinking skills. Ask:
  - What do I need to prioritize?
  - What do I need to learn?
  - What skills do I need to develop?
  - How should I communicate during the change process?
  - Who do I need to align myself with as we change?

When This Happens ...

You are trying hard to process the news about the merger, but you are still feeling uncertain and confused. What if Miami headquarters feels it is too expensive to continue your operation? What if they close your office? What if you lose your job? You have worked for this company for ten years. You have a family to support, a hefty mortgage payment, and other monthly expenses. Losing this job would be devastating.

Try This

Cut out two words from your vocabulary: *What if!* Asking yourself what if this and what if that will only lead to negative responses that will encourage you to resist the inevitable. Yes, Miami may close your operation. In life, anything can happen. Before you allow yourself to become mired in turmoil, kick into your problem-solving mode. Looking at this from a solution-oriented perspective will help you view the situation objectively. There is nothing you can do about the merger. Focus on what you can do to adapt to the news.

Working through major life changes earns personal badges of honor. Wear them proudly.

40. Help Yourself and Others Work Through Change

Becoming a quick-change artist does not mean you are immune to the feelings and emotions that come with change. Rather, it means that you recognize what you are feeling and know how to work through those feelings. Change means giving something up. When you give something up, you need to mourn your loss before you can move ahead. Even a welcome change, such as moving to a new home, will bring a sense of loss. After all, you are moving out of a home in which you built happy memories. Expect to feel both happy and sad. Feeling torn is normal as you move through change. Being aware of your emotions will enable you to help yourself and others move through the process.

Performance Prompts

- Help yourself and others through change by understanding the change process.
- Common phases of change are: denial, sadness, resistance, exploration, acceptance.
    - In denial, people have trouble accepting the change. This emotion may range from wishful thinking—*The merger could still fall through*—to complete refusal to believe the facts—*There is no way this will happen.*
    - As reality sets in, it is natural to feel sad. *Our company will never be the same. We'll lose the family atmosphere.* Feelings may range from slight sadness to an overwhelming sense of despair.
    - When people are sad, they resist the inevitable. A sense of turmoil may emerge. "Me-centered" emotions surface. *What's going to happen to me?*
    - Resistance paves the way to a more objective viewpoint. *The owner said our office isn't closing. It wouldn't make sense with our customer base.*

    - Objective thinking leads to exploration. *This merger might be a good thing. Being part of a larger corporation may bring new opportunities.*
    - The last phase of the change process is acceptance. *Whatever happens, I'll make the best of it.*
- Help others by analyzing where they are in the change process.
- Encourage everyone to talk. Listen well and show empathy and concern. Help others look at the situation objectively. When you see that they are accepting the change, help them look ahead to the end result and set goals for the future.

When This Happens . . .

One day your coworker, Colleen, says, "I heard some people saying they're going to close our office. I don't know what I'm going to do if I lose my job." Colleen is in the resistance phase, and you know it is preventing her from giving the level of customer service you expect.

Try This

"Colleen, it is scary to think that way. Think about this. We have a huge presence in the Northeast, our owner is staying on to run our branch, and Miami isn't going to want to risk losing our customer base." Colleen begins to look at the situation more objectively. "You're right. It wouldn't make sense to close our operation." You nod in agreement. "Let's focus on doing our jobs well. Everything will fall into place."

Let your coworkers and customers know they can count on you to be there for them.

41. Remain Objective

You are working to be a quick-change artist by understanding the phases of change and helping others who are struggling. Let's face it, though, you are human and may yourself fall back into feelings of confusion. Thoughts of *what's going to happen to me* may surface. It is time to talk to someone who can help you. One of the benefits of talking through a situation is that it helps you remain objective. When you find yourself thinking counterproductive thoughts, find someone to talk to—someone positive—who can help you.

Performance Prompts

- Talk. Get your feelings out in the open. The more you talk to others, the easier it will be for you to remain objective.
- Look at the change from all angles: the customer, the organization, the employees. Ask: *how will the change benefit each?*
- If your job is to present the change to your coworkers and customers, your first impulse may be to "sell" the change. Don't.
- Present both the positive and the negative sides. Encourage people to talk. Listen and respond truthfully. No phony sincerity. Avoid saying *"This is going to be great!"*
- Lower your expectations. During the change process realize that people are not going to function at their peak.
- Look for things that you can fix or make better. In other words, be a problem solver who looks problems in the face and deals with them.
- When you are beginning to lose your objectivity, ask yourself, *What opportunities are there to grow . . . to make things better . . . to shine . . . ?*
- Also ask yourself, *Can I control this situation?* If yes, do something about it. If no, stop worrying about things you cannot control.

When This Happens ...

One of your most profitable accounts is Don's Tuscan Grill. You need to inform Don about the merger. You want to assure him, but you do not want to make light of the situation.

Try This

Think about what you are going to say, and how Don might react. Consider saying, "Don, I'm calling to let you know about a company change. Effective July 1 we're merging with Omega Foods in Miami. While we undergo some internal changes, our primary goal is to conduct business as usual." Don immediately expresses concern about future food orders and deliveries. "I can understand your concern because we are your primary supplier. The corporate officers have assured us that our operation will not change. In fact, Mr. Thomas is staying on to run our branch." Don seems relieved. You follow up by saying, "We understand that any change is difficult, and our goal is to make this transparent for you. If you have any questions or concerns, please call me so we can discuss them." When you present a balanced perspective, your customers are going to appreciate your honesty. After all, change is a process for them too.

Put yourself in your customers' shoes to better understand their concerns.

42. Maintain an Upbeat Attitude

You already understand the importance of a positive attitude. That is easy when circumstances are good, but how do you remain positive and upbeat amid negative circumstances? Focus on the performance prompts below, and you will acquire valuable tools that will enable you to *always* remain positive, no matter what turmoil you are facing.

Performance Prompts

- Determine what type of person you are. Remember it is easier to be around people who maintain a positive attitude.
- Recognize that change is temporary, and focus forward to the end result.
- Keep up your morale. You—and only you—are in charge of you.
- Create a supportive environment. Supporting others will make them want to support you.
- Make others feel valued; it will keep you on a positive track.
- Give a compliment, a word of encouragement, a friendly smile every day.
- Always treat others the way you want to be treated.
- Give your customers extra care during periods of change. Remember that they, too, are experiencing your change. Stay close to them, pay attention, listen carefully, and make customer satisfaction your top priority.
- Caution: avoid being overly cheery during times of turmoil. People may begin to wonder about you! It's normal to be more reflective while undergoing change.
- Remember to always keep a healthy and realistic perspective. If you look at all sides objectively, you can remain positive and upbeat. It is all in the thoughts, words, and deeds you choose. Choose wisely.

When This Happens ...

Once again, the grapevine is growing. The lunch talk is taking an ugly, negative turn. You are trying hard to turn around the atmosphere by remaining positive. You talk to your lunch buddies objectively. You even worked through some possible scenarios to help them look at the situation realistically. Nothing is working.

Try This

Sometimes people just like to complain. They jump on the train to Negativeville and do not want to get off until they drag everyone around them onto the train. If you tried—but can't—turn around attitudes toward what is happening, then it is time for another change. If you decide that spending time away from the griping group is the best thing for you, then do it. Jump off that train. Avoid going to lunch with the group. Make other plans. Run errands. Be busy. Remember, especially during the change process, to always do what is best for you. You want to help others through change, but not at the expense of your mental health. If they ask you why you are not going with them anymore, be up front and tell them they are bringing you down too much.

Always avoid taking part in grapevine conversations.
Those grapes are almost always sour.

43. Stay Accountable for Outcomes

In times of turmoil and confusion, it is easy to let things slide. Deadlines may pass. Customer service may slip. Your energy level may wane. You may become easily distracted. When this happens, get yourself back on track by focusing. Focus on your customers. Focus on your work. Focus on your personal life. Staying focused on what is important will help you stay accountable for outcomes.

Performance Prompts

- Look beyond yourself at the big picture. Look ahead to the end result.
- Add value. Always give more than you take.
- During times of change, prioritize your work. Keep yourself on target until things return to a sense of normality.
- When goals and objectives are blurred during change, set short-term goals that will be more manageable.
- Set a personal goal to become a lifelong learner. Learning helps you keep on top of change.
- Get enough rest. Eat healthy foods. Exercise every day. Do what you can to keep your energy level consistent.
- Keep busy doing what is important and meaningful. Idle time can be dangerous. A wandering mind loses focus. Negative self-talk may bring you down.
- Stay tuned in to your customers, coworkers, and management. Talk to them more, and listen more. Ask others for suggestions, ideas, and input.
- Do not allow problems to get out of hand. When you see a problem developing, take care of it.
- Cut out the nonessentials during periods of change. Focus only on the necessary.

When This Happens . . .

Outside work, you are actively involved in a not-for-profit organization that provides tutoring to underprivileged children. At your monthly meeting, the executive director asks you to volunteer to take over the newsletter. You are thrilled until you start thinking about what is going on at work. Taking on this responsibility will require a huge time commitment.

Try This

Say, "Thank you for thinking of me. I'm definitely interested. I'll think it over to see if I can handle it right now, and I'll get back to you by Friday." You want to say yes, but as you weigh the pros and cons during the next few days, you decide that it is too much to take on with the impending merger. Right now, it is most important that you stay committed to doing your best at work during the change. Call the director, and say, "After giving this careful consideration, I'm going to have to decline because of work responsibilities. I appreciate that you considered me, and I hope I have another opportunity in the future." Before making a decision, take the time to think through the situation objectively. That way, you will make the right choice. Right now, the right choice is to concentrate on working through the change—and—continuing to do your best at work.

Rely on your common sense and good judgment to get you through any situation.

CHAPTER 7

TRAINING
Learn Your Lines

"If it wasn't hard, everyone would do it. It's the hard that makes it great."

—TOM HANKS

Tonight is opening night. The last rehearsal went well because Bob made sure Liz was prepared and knew her lines. She had spent so much time learning and watching the production that the transfer was seamless. You and the other cast members take your places on stage. You hear the audience applaud as the play is announced. The curtain rises, and the play begins. During Act I, only one of the actors, Mitch, flubs his lines. You quickly pick up on his mistake and ad lib until he is back on track. During Act II, Mitch misses his cue and another actor steps in for him. By Act III, you and the other actors are on edge wondering what is going on with Mitch. He almost makes it through Act III, but at the end he forgets his line yet again. The audience does not seem to notice; the members applaud wildly at the end of the play. You and the cast take your curtain calls, elated yet relieved that you made it through the first night. By the audience's reaction, you can tell that this play is going to be a hit. Bob gathers the cast together to congratulate all of you. He does not say anything about Mitch's performance but as you walk to the dressing rooms you overhear Bob asking Mitch to stay behind.

Before Mitch's performance problems become worse, Bob needs to find out the what is happening. Fortunately, the other actors covered for Mitch, but Bob needs to address the problem before it becomes more serious. The cast members will cover for a short time, but the members will become disgruntled if the situation persists performance after performance.

Good directors understand that a successful performance depends on cast members who know their lines thoroughly and have learned how to interact with their colleagues and the audience. When an actor performs poorly, the cause usually involves a lack of training or a lack of motivation. Bob made sure Mitch knew his lines, so now he is wondering if Mitch lacks the motivation to perform well. Still, before Bob reaches that conclusion, he needs to get Mitch's perspective. After all, his poor performance might simply be the result of first-night jitters or stage fright, both of which could be corrected through additional training.

Let's face it. In business, as in acting, it is important to learn your lines well. Unless you know what is expected, you cannot perform at your best. Your customers are going to suffer when you or your coworkers do not know how to find the best solution for them in every situation.

As a customer service star, begin by analyzing what you and your team need. What do you need to learn? What kind of training do you need? Think about all aspects of your job, from technical training to providing exceptional service to your customers. Learning one without the other will not create a satisfactory customer interaction. It is imperative that you learn all aspects of the job. In addition, understanding the big picture—your overall company operation and what your competition offers—will help you and your coworkers give your customers great performances every day.

"The only thing that you owe the public is a good performance."

—HUMPHREY BOGART

44. Analyze Training Needs

Before beginning any training program, you need to know the who, what, when, where, and how of your personal training needs. Who needs training? What kind of training is necessary? When should the training be completed? Where should the training occur? How should the training be done? By analyzing your training needs up front, you will become a successful trainer and learner.

Performance Prompts

From the trainer's perspective:

- Make a list of your training needs. For each employee, list strengths, areas of improvement, additional technical or job skills training needed, and additional customer service training needed.
- Include in your analysis training to use phone, electronic, and computer equipment.
- Test coworkers on their knowledge. Never assume they know what to do.

From the learner's perspective:

- Take responsibility for your own learning. Do not wait for your manager to recognize what you do not know. Tell your manager what training you need.
- Think about your job from a technical standpoint. What do you need to learn to do your job more effectively?
- Think about typical customer contacts you handle. What type of customer interactions are you uncomfortable handling?
- Make a list of all of your personal training needs.
- Prioritize your list, focusing on technical training first. To give great customer service, you have to know how to handle a customer's request.

- Talk to your manager to determine how and when you will receive your training.
- Together, set goals and dates for completion.

When This Happens . . .

Mrs. Harris received a sales flyer for air conditioning maintenance from your company, but she is not clear on exactly what is covered. For example, is damage caused by animals included? You are not sure either, not even after you review the clause on damage by animals on your computer. You try to talk your way through the problem by rephrasing the clause that is confusing her. She hangs up by saying, "I don't think I'm going to take this coverage. Thanks anyway." You do not feel comfortable about the way the conversation went, and you hope you do not get any more calls about the maintenance policy.

Try This

Whoa! Take responsibility for your own learning. Here is an opportunity for you to improve your skills, so take advantage of it. Talk to your manager, and ask for training. This is also a good time to make a quick analysis of any other training you might need.

The only way to truly satisfy customers
is to know how to satisfy them.

45. Learners Come in Different Styles

To be an effective learner, you must understand learning styles. Everyone has different buttons, different methods of learning, different strengths and weaknesses. Get to know your coworkers so that you will understand the best approach for each person—and learn what works best for you.

Performance Prompts

Learning Styles: You probably know that some types of training just do not work for you. Determining which type of learning works best for you will help your manager determine how best to train you.

- Some people are "let-me-see" learners, who learn through visualization. These types of learners easily understand written material, such as training guides, graphs, diagrams, and visual aids. Sometimes, they learn best independently.
- Some people are "tell-me" learners, who learn by listening. They learn best in instructor-led settings. Lectures, discussions, and question-and-answer sessions are effective tools.
- Some people are "show-me" learners, who need a hands-on experience. On-the-job training works best for these types of learners. Show them how to do the job by doing it. Show them what to say by saying it. Then have them do it or say it to ensure understanding.

For all learners: Training means absorbing new information. To make the most of any learning opportunity:

- Schedule short breaks every hour or two. Even a stand up, take a deep breath, and stretch break will boost energy and concentration.

- If you are allowed to eat and drink during training, choose high-energy foods like nuts, raisins, and juices.
- If you need a quick afternoon pick me up, boost your metabolism by eating a small piece of candy.
- For group training, vary the activities to accommodate different learning styles.
- Hold frequent discussions to break things up and energize the group.

When This Happens . . .

You explain to your manager, Jack, that you do not feel comfortable talking to customers about the new promotion flyer. You read the package, but it did not make much sense. This is not the way you learn best. You are a "tell-me" learner, who comprehends better when you hear the explanation.

Try This

Jack says, "Have a seat and we'll review it right now." Jack talks you through each step of the promotion. Then, he asks questions to ensure that you understood. "Thanks, Jack. I'm going to call Mrs. Harris back and explain it to her. She might change her mind and take the policy once she understands it clearly."

Take responsibility for learning.

46. Products, Services, and Company Policies

Before you can expect the people in your organization to provide outstanding customer service, they have to know *how* to give outstanding customer service. The only way for you and your coworkers to fully satisfy customers is to find the best solution for each of them. Giving every customer the same response is not going to solve every customer's problem. Being fully trained about products, services, and company policies, however, will enable you to find the best solution for each customer. What is right for one customer is not right for every customer.

Performance Prompts

- You cannot expect people to do the right thing unless they know what the right thing is.
- Devote adequate time to training coworkers to do the job they were hired to do.
- Train coworkers fully before allowing them to interact with customers.
- Stay with new employees or assign a coworker to work with them until they are comfortable doing the job independently.
- Periodically test your coworkers' knowledge. Never assume that people are going to remember everything.
- Train coworkers to be problem solvers. When everyone knows your products, services, and company policies well, you will all be armed with the knowledge to solve any customer's problem.
- Train coworkers to be good decision makers. To customers, you are your company. If you and your coworkers are well trained, you will be able to help customers reach the decision that is right for them.
- When you are completely familiar with your products and services, you will know how to solve problems and make

good decisions. This is going to help you generate sales, adding to your company's bottom line.

- Make sure everyone knows how to properly use phone, electronic, and computer equipment.

When This Happens . . .

Jack has an "aha" moment. If one employee does not understand the new promotion flyer, how many others do not understand it? That employee mentioned she lost a sale because she was unsure about the coverage. Jack manages nine service employees who are responsible for incoming phone calls from customers. It is time for a fast check.

Try This

Make a quick analysis by testing everyone's knowledge and comfort level in explaining the package. Jack creates a simple worksheet. As he questions the employees, he checks their responses. Of the nine employees, four have misunderstood parts of the package. Jack recognizes that Lisa is a "show-me" learner, so he coaches her as she talks to a customer. For the other three, he reviews the material and questions them on their understanding. Now Jack is comfortable that every employee understands the material.

Knowledgeable employees are credible employees.

47. General Steps to Exceptional Customer Service

Once employees have completed their technical training, it is time to train them to give great customer service. Such training begins with the general steps that every employee in every business needs to know to provide outstanding customer service.

Performance Prompts

The general steps are:

- Make a great first impression.
    - Smile. Make eye contact. Maintain an open, relaxed demeanor. Keep your facial expressions friendly. Dress appropriately, and be properly groomed for your occupation.
- Project a positive attitude.
    - Be helpful, interested, trustingwothy, reassuring, and reliable. Speak respectfully. Believe in yourself and then believe that you can make a difference. Keep an open mind by not stereotyping people.
- Communicate effectively.
    - Tune in and focus. Be courteous. Listen completely. Think before you speak. Speak clearly. Use correct grammar. Make sure your tone and facial expressions match the message you are sending. Listen more than you speak.
- Build and maintain relationships.
    - Build a rapport with customers. Ask questions to find the best solutions. Find the right solution for each particular customer. Remember customers' names and faces. Make each customer feel valued.

Think, also, about customer service when talking on the phone or communicating online.

- Smile when you speak. Maintain a helpful and interested tone of voice. Stay tuned in to your customers by listening completely. Answer e-mail queries promptly. Respond to your customers' needs. Put a human touch into your writing.

When This Happens . . .

You paid close attention and wrote notes when you received your customer service training. It is a subject that is important to you. Without customers, you would not be needed. You get it! Today you noticed that when a customer came into your business, your coworker, Staci, did not make a great first impression. She did not look up, did not smile, and when the customer asked her a question she answered in a bored tone without making eye contact.

Try This

It is terrific that you understand the importance of treating customers well. You know that customer service begins with making a great first impression. But unless your coworkers get it, you are going to lose customers. Talk to Staci. Share what you observed. Explain how she appeared from the customer's perspective. Help her to understand that it takes all of you to give great customer service.

You only get one chance to make a first impression.
Make a great one.

48. Specific Steps to Exceptional Customer Service

Understanding the general steps to giving great customer service is crucial. Knowing how to present yourself well by making a positive first impression, maintaining a good attitude, communicating well, and building relationships forms the basis to making a lasting impression in your customers' minds. Now it is time to focus on the specific steps you must take for your particular business. The customer who is shopping for a cell phone has different needs than the customer who is shopping for a phone system for a call center operation. Knowing your customers, their needs, and how you can best respond to them will set you apart from your competition.

Performance Prompts

Think about the needs of your customers. Formulate specific steps from a customer service perspective that your employees should take to:

- Greet customers and make them feel valued.
    - How should you greet each customer when they come in or call?
    - What should you say or do after greeting customers?
- Help customers and find the right solutions.
    - What questions should you ask to understand your customers' needs?
    - What information do you need to obtain to find the best solution?
    - How should you communicate with each customer? What specific things do you need to tell/ask them?
- End transactions in a way that ensures customer satisfaction.
    - What should you say to make sure the customer is satisfied?
    - How should you end contacts?

The answers to these questions will be different for each business but it is crucial that you know the specifics. Unless you learn and train how to handle each step of a typical customer transaction, you cannot assume your coworkers will know what to do.

When This Happens . . .

It is your responsibility to come up with a customer interaction framework for your coworkers. You know how to give great service but how do you translate that to your coworkers? And how do you put it on paper?

Try This

It is not that difficult. Just answer the questions above. The greeting and ending may be as simple as *Hi, my name is ___, how may I help you?* to *Thanks for coming in. We appreciate your business.* When formulating responses about helping the customer and finding the right solution, think about a typical customer interaction. Your framework may be pretty basic to quite involved. It all depends on what you need to know and what you need to communicate to find the best solution for each customer. When you cover your coworkers, stress that this is only a framework; they should always personalize contacts and treat each customer as an individual. Giving the same answer to every customer makes you seem like a robot.

Find ways to give your customers more than they expect.

49. Conduct Market Research

As the direct link to customers, you and your coworkers are in the best position to conduct market research. Think about it. Who else can provide better data than the source you are studying? Your customers! Learn and then train your coworkers how to research your customers, and you will gain a valuable source of raw data.

Performance Prompts

Learn how to conduct basic market research:

- Observe and listen to customers as they shop in your store, come into your place of business, or call you on the phone. What do their attitudes say about your business?
- Get to know your customers, and find out why they come to you.
- Pay attention. Listen closely. Customers will tell you what they need from you.
- When customers make purchases, ask how they are going to use the products.
- Make a list of customer comments—what they do like, and what they would like.

Initiate a customer survey and feedback system:

- Do this through comment cards, follow-up calls, or mail/e-mail surveys.
- Ask specific, open-end questions that require more than a yes or no answer.
    - *What do you like best about our company?*
    - *What don't we do that you would like us to do?*
    - *How well do our employees meet your needs in:*
        - *Greeting you?*
        - *Answering your questions completely and accurately?*

    - *Helping you find the right solution?*
    - *Making sure you are completely satisfied?*
- *What can we do to improve our service to you?*

When you receive response data:

- Pay attention to customer feedback.
- Analyze responses.
- Act on viable suggestions for improvement.

When This Happens . . .

You trained your coworkers to conduct a short survey at the end of phone calls by asking *what can we do to improve our service to you?* They are to note the responses on the form you provided and turn the forms in daily.

Try This

At the end of the week, you begin to see a trend. Most customers are satisfied with your company, but seven were unhappy with the installation date policy and one did not like the music when placed on hold. You realize it is time to analyze what can be done to improve installation time frames. By asking your customers what you can do to improve, you will be able to identify trends, set goals, correct problem areas, monitor your progress, and most importantly, stay close to your customers.

When you act on suggestions for improvement,
you will develop a loyal customer base.

50. Understand the Big Picture

What is the big picture? It is your entire business operation: your coworkers, every department and branch in your company, and even your competition. You give customers your best when you understand the big picture. Knowing your own job is not enough to give great customer service. You also need to understand how everyone works together for your customers. Otherwise, you may not be able to give customers exactly what they need. Remember, though, your customers see you as the big picture. They do not care if you need to call another department to check on something or if the problem was someone else's fault. They are speaking to you, and you are the only picture they see.

Performance Prompts

- You will have more respect for your coworkers if you understand what they do and how your jobs, roles, and departments interrelate.
- Take responsibility to learn about your entire organization and how the departments relate to each other.
- Learn all you can about your competition. You will gain a better understanding of your products or services when you know what else is out there.
- Whenever you speak with customers, take responsibility for your entire company. Use *I* or *we,* rather than *they. I'm sorry we made a mistake* sounds better than *I'm sorry they made a mistake.* The customer really does not care who *they* are.
- Whenever you implement a company change, make sure all your coworkers fully understand the change and why it is being implemented before expecting them to talk to customers about it.
- Learn to be solution oriented. Before asking someone else to solve problems, see if you can come up with a good solution. Take responsibility.

- Teach your coworkers to solve their own problems. Before you readily give them the answer to a problem, ask them some leading questions to see if they can come up with a viable solution. Ask *what do you think you should do?*
- Think outside the box. Think of new and unusual solutions.

When This Happens . . .

Almost every day you need to call your dispatch department to check on a customer's installation time. You become frustrated when the employees put you on hold for a couple minutes. You are sure they are goofing off at your expense, and today a customer blasted you for leaving him on hold so long while you checked.

Try This

Wouldn't it help if you understood what the dispatchers do? Tell your boss you would like to know more about their operation so you can understand why they put you on hold for so long. After receiving a tour of their department, you realize that they need to call the installer before they can answer you. Next time you have to put a customer on hold, you will have a mental snapshot of the big picture. "Mr. Customer, I'm going to check with my dispatch department. They'll need to contact the installer so it's going to take me a few minutes. Is that all right?"

Take responsibility for being your company's spokesperson.

51. Handle Customer Complaints

Working in customer service would be great if you did not have to deal with customer complaints, right? Think how pleasant your job would be if you only encountered happy customers who love everything you do. Now that's dreaming, isn't it? The truth is that in customer service, as in life, you will deal with people who are not happy. When you work in customer service, your job includes handling customers well—and that means handling all customers confidently in any situation.

Performance Prompts

Whenever you encounter a customer who is upset, angry, or complaining, determine:

- Why is the customer upset?
  - Listen actively to what the customer is saying. Do not interrupt.
  - Focus on the problem, not the person.
  - Stay calm and composed even if the customer is angry or upset.
  - View the situation from the customer's perspective.
  - Assure the customer you will take care of the problem.
- What caused the problem?
  - Restate the problem to make sure you understand it correctly.
  - Research to identify the root cause of the problem.
  - Think about how you can resolve this.
- What can I say to make things right with the customer?
  - Apologize. It is the right thing to do when a customer is upset.
  - Display empathy. Put yourself in the customer's shoes.
  - Appreciate the customer for giving you the chance to make things right.

- What is the best solution I can offer the customer?
  - Explain what you are going to do to correct the situation.
  - Tell the customer what you *can* do rather than what you *can't* do.
  - Avoid assigning blame, either to the customer or to another employee.
  - If you have no clue what to do or if your recommendation is not satisfactory, work with the customer to find a viable solution.
- What do we need to do to keep this from happening again?
  - Follow up to make sure the customer is satisfied with the resolution.
  - Analyze what went wrong.
  - Fix what needs to be fixed.

When This Happens . . .

You answer a call from an upset customer. She is yelling into the phone, and you find your stomach knotting up.

Try This

Remember that she is not angry at you. Follow the performance prompts step by step to figure out what happened and how you can resolve the problem. By calming yourself and not taking her anger personally, you are in a better position to listen well, analyze what went wrong, and find the best solution.

When a customer complains,
look at it as an opportunity to improve.

52. Learning Is a Continual Project

Learning never stops. You learn something every day. You may have to learn something new or learn how to do the old in a new way. Be a good learner. Also be a good teacher. Tell, show, demonstrate, help, stand behind, nudge, and offer encouragement. And do not just do any of these once. Teaching, as well as learning, is continual.

Performance Prompts

- Look for learning opportunities. When you learn, you grow.
- Ask questions so you can learn more.
- Look for better ways to do things.
- Do not expect people to give you answers. Do your research before going to someone else for the answer.
- When you go to your boss with a problem, also go with a proposed solution.
- Look for teaching opportunities. Share your knowledge with others.
- Let your coworkers know exactly what you expect of them.
- Train coworkers on the behaviors you expect them to display.
- If you cannot answer someone's question, be up front and say so. Follow up with *I'll find out.*
- Share what is going on in your workplace with your coworkers. Be as open as you can be.
- Think of your place of employment as your business. Think of yourself as the owner when making decisions. Ask *what would I do if this were my business?*
- Try to come up with ways to improve your company operations.
- Offer concrete suggestions for improvement.

When This Happens . . .

Your manager announced in a meeting that everyone in your work group must complete a new computer-based training program on customer service. You really do not want to go to another of these classes. You have been to so many classes in the past you feel you could teach them. Besides, you already give great customer service. After the meeting, you tell a coworker, "What a waste of time. I really don't want to go to this thing. Two days out of the office means I'm going to be slammed with work." He nods in agreement.

Try This

Back up! Before you develop a bad attitude about training, think about this. Complaining infuses you with negativity. Rather than griping about the inevitable, change your self-talk. Tell yourself that you might just learn a thing or two from this class. If you look for opportunities to learn something, they will present themselves. Be open to learning. Any learning. As for spending two days away from your work, look at the time away from work as time to rejuvenate and come back armed with new knowledge.

Learn from your experiences—good or bad.

CHAPTER 8

TEAMWORK
The Actors Make the Cast

"You have five seconds to enjoy it,
and then you remember who you didn't thank."
—HELEN HUNT

After three nights of Mitch flubbing his lines and missing his cues, the cast members are grumbling about having to pull his weight. "The rest of us know our lines. Why should we have to cue him all the time?" "Yeah, why isn't Bob doing anything about it?" "It isn't right. Each of us is responsible for our part—except for Mitch. He just doesn't seem to care." Bob asks the cast to stay for a short meeting. Everyone, except Mitch, gathers backstage. "First, I want to thank you for the great job you've done so far. I also want to thank each of you for helping Mitch. I hoped that he could pull things together by now, but he hasn't been able to. Before talking to you, I asked Mitch if it was all right for me to share what's going on, and it's OK with him. Right before our first performance, he found out that his sister has been diagnosed with a serious illness and will require a lot of care." You and the rest of the cast immediately go from griping to concern for Mitch and his sister. This changes the whole picture. "Mitch didn't want to say or do anything to upset the play, and he wants to stay with the production. I'm confident that once he works through this problem, he'll perform as he did in rehearsals. I'm sharing this news with you because it's not right for you to wonder what's going on. We need to stick together as a team and help Mitch through this tough time." All of you assure Bob that you will do whatever it takes to help Mitch.

Bob shared Mitch's news with the cast because he sensed the members were becoming disgruntled for doing more than their share. Can you imagine, if Bob had not said anything? The entire production would have suffered because the actors were tired of Mitch's poor performance. Not only did Bob share the news with the cast, he thanked them for helping Mitch. He stressed the importance of working together to assist Mitch until he gets back on track. Because Bob communicated the news to the group and stressed the need for teamwork, the actors were willing to pull together.

What does team building have to do with customer service? Customer service stars, who encourage open communication and work to build strong teams, achieve better results. When you and your coworkers pull together, you will challenge each other to do your best, to consistently perform well, and to provide a high level of customer service.

It is true that two can do it better than one, as long as the two are working toward the same goals. As a customer service star, you can ensure all of you are working toward the same goals by developing your group into a united team, one in which everyone works together, supports each other, and strives to achieve the team goals.

Teams do not develop by themselves, though. It requires a commitment that begins with strong leadership. Establishing a team identity, creating a supportive environment, expecting everyone to be team players, and continually analyzing how to make things better is the glue that forms a cohesive team.

"We're here for a reason. I believe a bit of the reason is to throw little torches out to lead people through the dark."

—WHOOPI GOLDBERG

53. Strong Teams = Success

Why should you be concerned with developing a team if you already have coworkers who do their jobs and meet company goals and objectives? Why would you want to rock the boat when things are going smoothly? Even though you may be sailing smoothly, you need to prepare yourself for stormy seas. When that happens, do you and your coworkers work together effectively? Or do you swim in different directions, each trying to stay afloat? When the going gets tough, do you continue giving high quality customer service? Or do you flounder and falter? Think about how you spend your days. Are your team members self-sufficient or do they come to you to solve their problems? Think about the advantages that will result if you invest the time to train your coworkers to stand together, united as one team, to achieve company goals and provide outstanding customer service.

Performance Prompts

- Developing a strong, self-supportive, committed team initially requires a large time commitment, but the pay off is huge, particularly in terms of freeing up time later on.
- Positive leaders understand the importance of developing leadership in others.
- The characteristics of strong teams are:
    - They have a strongly defined mission.
    - They share common goals.
    - They openly communicate with each other in a positive, constructive manner.
    - They respect each other.
    - They trust each other.
    - They have effective leadership, both within the group and by the person managing the group.
    - All members are encouraged to actively participate.
    - Well-defined conflict resolution procedures are in place.

- Well-defined decision making procedures are in place.
- There is a strong focus on objectives, achievements, and improvement.
- The group establishes ground rules for everyone to follow.

When This Happens . . .

Your manager, who covers two offices, asks you to become team leader for your office. "I've heard from another manager that the employees aren't working together, that there's even been some infighting. I've depended on you in the past when I needed something done, and I'm depending on you now to turn things around before they get out of hand." While you appreciate her vote of confidence, you wonder how you are going to accomplish this. There is some infighting; in fact, there is no team spirit whatsoever. You do not think there is any hope for your group.

Try This

Do not give up before you try. Understanding the characteristics of strong teams will help you define where you are and where you need to go.

Build a strong team. You can't do it all alone.

54. Establish a Team Identity

How do you turn a group of coworkers into a team? Start by establishing a team identity. Take a *We,* not *Me,* approach. Erase the words *I* and *You* from your vocabulary. Start building rapport with the team as a whole. Compliment members of the team when you see them building team rapport with each other. Always emphasize the team—team efforts, team achievements, team areas of improvement—rather than referring to the individual members of the team.

Performance Prompts

- Make it a habit of always saying *we,* not *you* or *I.*
- Use the words *our team* when talking to your coworkers.
- Encourage a respectful environment by respecting others first.
- Build a climate of trust by showing your coworkers that you trust them.
- Encourage open communication by being a good listener, by using positive language, and by expecting the same from others.
- Keep all team members informed.
- Tell coworkers specifically what is expected of the team.
- Share responsibility for team building with your entire team.
- Create an enthusiastic, positive work environment by including everyone when making team decisions, solving team problems, and resolving team conflict.
- Reward team building behavior.
- Set team goals together.
- Discuss areas of improvement with your team.
- Emphasize and recognize team achievements.

When This Happens . . .

After speaking with your boss, you wonder why you agreed to work on team building. Sherry does not talk to Gavin. Ben and

Keith argue with each other almost every day. Two of your coworkers like to stir things up, and the other four just try to do their jobs and stay away from the problems. You have a lot of work to do to try to change this environment. How do you even begin?

Try This

Take things one small step at a time. Get used to thinking of your coworkers as your teammates. Picture your team working together. Start using the words *we* and *our team* whenever you talk to your coworkers. Using these words creates a mental picture of your team as one entity. Discourage troublemakers by stopping them when they talk negatively about each other. Take a *we're in this together* approach. Ask your responsible coworkers to help stop the negative behavior when they see it. By starting small and not expecting things to change overnight, you will see things change. Try team building exercises. For example, you could hold a team problem-solving meeting. Or, you could ask Sherry and Gavin to work together on a project. Look for opportunities to compliment your coworkers when you see them take a team approach.

There is no "I" in Team.

55. Foster a Supportive Environment

First, think of your coworkers as a united team. Then, create a work environment that supports all members of your team. When you are supportive of your coworkers, they are more apt to be supportive of you. Behaviors rub off: good or bad. Adopt positive and constructive behaviors. When you do, your coworkers are likely to adopt them too.

Performance Prompts

- Look for opportunities to help others.
- Be someone others can come to for help in solving problems and reaching decisions.
- Ask what you can do to help others rather than looking for what others can do to help you.
- If someone asks for your help and you cannot help immediately, set up a time when you can.
- Expect your coworkers to help others. When you see these behaviors, thank your coworkers for pitching in.
- Promote an environment of open communication.
- Listen well to each member of your team.
- Think before you speak to make sure that what you are about to say is constructive.
- Speak clearly, and then be open to discussion and questions.
- Give credit to coworkers for team accomplishments. *We did it.*
- Take personal responsibility for team mistakes. *I'm sorry, I made a mistake.*
- Hold team meetings. Encourage participation by all members.
- Consider any question or statement as valuable. Always respect the speaker.
- Laughing in the workplace can enthuse your team, as long as you are laughing together, *with* each other.

- Laughing at your coworkers' expense is never supportive.
- When conflicts arise, work to resolve the issue before it gets out of hand.

When This Happens . . .

Things are beginning to improve. After completing a project together, Sherry and Gavin are speaking now. Slowly, your coworkers are referring to *us* and using *we* when speaking about the group. But, you want to see more progress. How can you achieve this?

Try This

Try another team-building activity. When a member of your team has a problem, adopt a *how can we help* approach. It is important that you take an active role in helping others; your team members will then emulate this behavior. So, give your team members the opportunity to help. Next time one of your coworkers asks for your help in solving a problem, involve the team. Together, come up with the best solution and give credit to the team.

Acknowledge positive behaviors immediately and always give credit to others.

56. Form a Cohesive and United Team

Building a team that effectively works together is a change process that involves several stages. You are not only changing the way you operate, you are also changing your mindset and behaviors. As team leader, you will guide your coworkers to open communication, a spirit of cooperation, team creativity, and cohesiveness.

Performance Prompts

Stage 1: Communication

- Encourage an atmosphere of open communication. Share what is going on and explain *why*. Ask, rather then tell, when you need something done. Clearly outline the team's mission, plan, and goals, so that you gain team support. Talk about team progress and achievements. Together, work through conflicts and solve problems. Talk to each other. Get to know your team members on a personal basis.

Stage 2: Cooperation

- Open communication develops into trust and respect among team members. You will see your team helping and cooperating with each other. Delegate more responsibility to them, but first, clearly define your expectations and provide training. Be available to help and support. Set up your team to succeed and, when they do, acknowledge their successes, show your appreciation, and praise team efforts.

Stage 3: Creativity

- Close relationships and camaraderie develop from a cooperative team effort. Members will begin to work through problems and conflicts effectively with minimal assistance.

Your team will start taking responsibility for its success. When this happens, the members will also want to have a say in how to reach team goals. Encourage an atmosphere of creative thinking, and teach them how to set goals. Now, you need to learn how to let go and allow your team the independence to try things its own way. Allow the members to make mistakes, then guide them back on track.

Stage 4: Cohesion

- Your team reaches this stage when goals are achieved, team members come to you less often for help, it is easier to delegate work, progress continues in your absence, people outside your team give you positive feedback, and morale and commitment are high. Your main role now is to be your team's cheerleader and coach. Cheerlead when they succeed. Coach when you see them getting off track. Continue to work on all four stages to ensure your team remains united.

When This Happens . . .

This seems like a lot to do. How do you spend adequate time building a strong and committed team *and* doing your own work? It might be too much to expect.

Try This

Think about it from a different perspective. Yes, you will need to devote a lot of time to this goal, but think of the end result. You will have more time to do your work because your team will be self-sufficient, take more responsibility, and work autonomously. It all begins with open, positive, and constructive communication.

Cohesiveness is the glue that binds.

57. Strengthen Your Team by Being a Team Player

No good director has ever developed an award-winning cast and then left them alone during the run of the play. If cohesiveness is the glue that binds, you must strive to make sure the glue stays strong. Whether you are the manager, a team leader, or a team member, every person must work together for the team to succeed. Take responsibility for yourself and for your team. Monitor, support, encourage, and steer your team to success.

Performance Prompts

- Never be above doing any job. Be the first to volunteer.
- Always show your appreciation for a job well done.
- Give credit where credit is due.
- Gain respect by first respecting others.
- Commit yourself to your team. Be loyal to your coworkers.
- Never allow yourself or your team members to become complacent.
- Set the bar high when setting team goals. What you expect is what you are going to get, both from yourself and others.
- Be a team booster by keeping a smile on your face, being sincere, staying actively involved in your team, maintaining an environment of mutual support, and keeping your energy level consistently high.
- Before judging your team members, put yourself in their shoes.
- Let your team know they can depend on you.
- Do something every day to let your team members know you value them.
- Remember to value your high-performance team members. Never take anyone for granted.
- Do something every day to break the routine and have some fun.
- Do something every day to make your team members feel good about coming to work.

When This Happens . . .

You feel great about your team's progress. You spent a lot of time encouraging open communication, developing a spirit of cooperation, showing coworkers how to become more creative, and observing your team become cohesive and united. You are proud of them, and you are pleased with yourself for investing the time and effort. It definitely was worth every minute you spent.

Try This

It is time to celebrate. You worked hard to develop your group into a self-sufficient team. They also worked hard during this change process. Reward your accomplishments. Break your new routine and have some fun. Think about what you can do for your coworkers to show your appreciation. Treat them to lunch or breakfast. Host a sporting event or take your team to a hometown game. Tell each of them specifically what you admire about them and how important they are to you.

A word of encouragement is a powerful tool.

58. Analyze What You Can Do to Improve

When you reach the cohesion stage of team building, it is easy to become complacent. Perhaps you feel you deserve a break. Your team is coming to you with problems less often. The members are making their own decisions. They are setting personal team goals that surpass company goals. You see your role now as their cheerleader and coach. When they succeed, you praise them. When they start getting off track, you guide them back. It is nice having extra time to do your own work without interruption. *How long are things going to stay this way?* Now that you have extra time, make time for regular review and analysis. Unless you review and analyze, you will not know what you can improve.

Performance Prompts

- Ask for ideas and suggestions from each team member.
- Be open to their ideas and suggestions, and act on practical ones.
- Stay actively involved in conflict-resolution and problem-solving meetings.
- In meetings, encourage everyone to participate and listen closely to what people say.
- Foster an environment of independent thinking, and listen receptively when coworkers bring you their input.
- Respect everyone's right to differing opinions. Good ideas are often borne out of a difference of opinion.
- Monitor your mission and plan. Update them when you need to make changes.
- Monitor your team goals. When you reach them, set new goals.
- Look at all areas to see what can be improved.
- When new employees join your team, spend time integrating them into your team. Work with the new and existing

coworkers on each step of team building, and monitor their progress.

- When implementing new procedures, work through the change process, but understand that with change may come a breakdown in team cohesiveness. Work to bring the team back to a high level of cooperation.

When This Happens . . .

Things were running smoothly until you implemented a change in work assignments. You trained coworkers in the new procedures, but production has slipped and your team seems out of focus.

Try This

The four stages of team building are communication, cooperation, creativity, and cohesion. There is, however, one additional stage—continuance. It is up to you to keep your team cohesive. The only way to achieve this is to keep assessing the team's performance. As necessary, go back to an earlier stage of team building and move forward again. Try to find out why team members seem out of focus. Then, help them become a cohesive team again.

Never become complacent.
Always be on the lookout for ways to improve.

CHAPTER 9

MOTIVATION
Monitoring the Process

"I've often said, the only thing standing between me and greatness is me."

—WOODY ALLEN

The play is in its second week. With everyone's help, Mitch pulled himself together and is performing well. Other than the occasional glitches, the production is smooth. At least you and the rest of the cast think so. Since the meeting about Mitch, Bob has not said anything to any of you about your performances. You assume you are doing a good job, but are you? What does Bob think? What does the audience think? Unless someone gives you feedback, you must rely on your own assumptions. You and the other cast members motivate each other with praise. After tonight's performance, Bob calls a cast meeting. "I want to tell you what a great job you've done so far. I've been paying close attention to how the play is going, and I'm so proud of each of you. You've pulled together as a team, and it shows in every performance. Tonight all of you performed exceptionally well. I watched the audience's reactions, and their faces told me how great you're doing, too. Thank you, each and every one of you. Keep up the terrific work. I know you'll continue to perform your best." You breathe a mental sigh of relief. Now, you want to do even better. All this time you wondered if Bob noticed, and he did. Bob was busy observing the process. On the way out, the cast members agree. Even even though you thought you were doing well, it felt great hearing it from Bob.

By telling the cast members how they are doing, Bob is motivating them to continue to perform well. Imagine if Bob had not observed how the play was going. Suppose he did not understand the importance of complimenting the cast. How long do you think the actors' desire to do well would last? Because Bob paid close attention to the cast, as well as to the audience, he knew specifically what to say to motivate the actors.

Customer service stars understand the importance of observing what is going on in the workplace. That is the only way to know if everyone is consistently providing exceptional customer service. Most people want to perform their best, yet everyone needs motivation. When you observe your coworkers, you will learn how to motivate them.

When you get into your customer service role at work, get fully into it. Be a hands-on performer. Know what is going on. Stop, look, and listen to your coworkers' performances. When you pay attention, you will know the level of customer service the team is providing. Document what you see, as your memory may not be as perfect as you think. By evaluating your coworker's performances, you will know how to motivate them to continue to do their best. Always be on your best behavior to show others that you are united with them in giving exceptional customer service.

"As for me, prizes are nothing. My prize is my work."

—KATHARINE HEPBURN

59. Hands-On Customer Service

As a result of your training and learning, you formed a cohesive team in which everyone strives to do their personal best. Now, how do you keep everyone, including yourself, performing at that level? By being there. You cannot be a customer service star unless you spend time with your team. When with your team, think about this: your coworkers are also your customers. Treat them the way you want them to treat your customers. Give individual attention. Spend quality time, listen, and respond to their needs.

Performance Prompts

- Unless you observe, you will not know how well your team is satisfying customers.
- No matter your role, commit to being part of the day-to-day operation.
- Make being there a high priority, daily task, even if just for a few minutes each day.
- Make your attitude *I'll make time now,* rather than *I'll get to it later.*
- When you are there, give the situation your undivided attention.
- Spend time with coworkers individually. Ask how they are doing, and find out in what areas they need help. If you ask, they will tell you.
- Talk about customer service when you are with your team.
- Communicate customer service goals to your coworkers, and make certain they understand those goals.
- Treat everyone as though they are your customers. That will keep you focused in the right direction.

When This Happens . . .

You do not see how you can spend time with your coworkers this week. Every day is filled. Today is your all-day planning meeting. Tomorrow you have a crucial project to complete. On Wednesday you are participating in a conference call about changes to your ordering process. On Thursday you are training a new employee. On Friday, you are meeting with your boss to discuss customer service results. Then you have daily reports, follow ups, reading and responding to e-mail, phone calls, and customer escalations. There is no way you can squeeze any more time out of your schedule. Next week looks better for spending time with your coworkers.

Try This

Don't have the time? Too busy this week? Think about the consequences of delaying your most important job. Your coworkers might think customer service is not important to you and slack off. As a result, your customer service results will start to slip. You will handle more customer escalations because your coworkers are no longer doing their best. You will have less time to spend working on crucial projects, reading e-mail, making follow up calls, and so on. Commit to spend time every day with your coworkers. Allow someone else to train the new employee. Take a shorter lunch. Even if you can only spend fifteen minutes a day with your team, your coworkers will appreciate your attention and will know that you value them.

When scheduling your time,
make being there your top priority.

60. Take Charge: Stop, Look, and Listen

Make the time you spend with your coworkers count, especially if you only have a few minutes. You may just want to catch up on your coworkers' personal lives, as this kind of interest is also part of team building. Still, keep these conversations short so that you can pay attention to your most important goal: motivating everyone to give exceptional customer service.

Performance Prompts

- Expect everyone, including yourself, to do your best.
- Step up and lead your team to excellence.
- Stop what you are doing when you have an opportunity to observe customer contacts.
- Look and listen. Pay complete attention to both good and poor performances.
- Be aware of how your customers are responding.
- Assess the situation.
- When you see a situation that needs immediate correction, do it immediately.
- Never ignore poor performance hoping it will correct itself. It will not.
- If you ignore a poor performance, your coworkers are going to notice. Their performances may also begin to slip.
- Always treat your coworkers the way you expect them to treat your customers.
- Make sure customer service is important to you. When it is important to you, it will be important to your coworkers.

When This Happens . . .

You scheduled blocks of time every day this week to spend with your coworkers. Today you are taking only a quick lunch break to make this work. When you ask Theresa how she is doing, she starts describing her crazy weekend. Her story is funny, but as you are listening, you overhear Jeremy talking on the phone to a customer. You do not want to cut Theresa off, yet you want to hear what Jeremy is saying. How do you listen to Theresa while observing Jeremy?

Try This

You can't. It is impossible to pay complete attention to two things at once. If you try to listen to both, you will listen to neither well. While it is important to share a fun moment with Theresa, your number one goal is to observe work performance. Ask Theresa to hold that thought. Give your attention to Jeremy. After you observe his customer contact, go back to Theresa and thank her for waiting. Let all of your coworkers know that you are going to spend time with each of them, but your first priority is always to pay attention to the level of customer service they are providing.

When customers are number one with you,
you set a great example.

61. Document Your Observations

Why document your observations? You already have a busy schedule and finding the time to be with your team is difficult enough. You think you will remember everything, but will you, particularly if you get bogged down with other tasks? Unless you document what you see and hear, you will be surprised at what gets lost. When you need to provide feedback or appraisals, you will appreciate documentation. A word of caution, however: only document your direct observations. When coworkers relate their observations, thank them, and make a note to follow up to see if the behavior is repeated.

Performance Prompts

- Documentation is important for spotting trends and patterns, commending good performance, correcting poor behavior, and preparing appraisals.
- Documentation provides a reference point for individual feedback.
- Without documentation, you probably will not remember certain specific details weeks or months from now.
- Look for strengths as well as weaknesses.
- Document anything out of the ordinary, both positive and negative.
- Documentation helps you correct inappropriate behaviors before they turn into bad habits.
- Specific situations warrant documentation, including your observations of coworkers, customer escalations in which a coworker's behavior resulted in a customer complaint, customer commendations, and company commendations.
- When preparing documentation, include the following key points: date, time (if applicable), coworker name, and a description of your specific observation. If you speak with a coworker about her performance, document your conversation and the agreed-upon action, if appropriate.

When This Happens . . .

Your observation confirms that Jeremy provides good customer service. He handled the phone call with his customer well, as you expected. Before ending the call, he said, "I'm really happy that I had the chance to talk to you today. My name is Jeremy, and I'm here to help you if you have any questions or need anything else. Thanks for choosing our business." Because the call was routine, you do not make any notes, but you thought the way Jeremy ended the call was exceptionally good.

Try This

The purpose of observing is to monitor overall performance in an effort to correct problems and praise good performance. You and your coworkers are expected to end phone conversations by thanking the customer for calling. The way Jeremy ended his call was not ordinary. He did more than say *thanks for calling*. What he said was heartfelt and made the customer feel valued. Make a note of this. When it comes time to motivate your team, you can praise Jeremy and share this specific example. When it comes time for personal feedback and appraisals, you will have a record of specific examples of behavior.

Documenting performance keeps you on top of things.

62. Motivate Your Team

One of your most important tasks as a customer service star is to motivate your coworkers. Motivation occurs when people feel good about their jobs. Motivation encourages people to strive to achieve more and do better. If accomplishments go unnoticed, the drive to achieve wanes. People want to hear a word of encouragement. People want someone to notice when they perform well. People want to know their efforts matter. That goes for everyone. It is human nature to want to be noticed and recognized. The best form of motivation is recognition, and you can only give recognition when you know what is going on.

Performance Prompts

- Give group recognition, and thank your team when the members perform well.
- When giving recognition or saying thanks, offer specific details.
- Be sincere when saying thanks and giving recognition. Too much of anything may begin sounding phony or ho-hum and will lose its impact.
- Never underestimate the power of a word of encouragement. Or a smile. Or a pat on the back. Or a thumbs up. . . . You get the idea.
- Motivate your best performers. Do not take them for granted.
- Recognize customer service accomplishments, by both individuals and the team as a whole.
- Motivate with recognition, awards, and compensation.
- Recognize positive accomplishments during a meeting or by posting a notice on a bulletin board, providing a coworker with a designated parking space for the month. . . . Reward coworkers by treating your team to breakfast, buying a box of candy, giving a gift certificate. . . . Compensate

an individual with an hour off with pay, allowing an extended lunch hour, giving a small bonus. . . .

- Caution: there is a danger in motivating with rewards and compensation. Be careful that the rewards do not become the reason your coworkers strive to achieve. The best motivation is a feeling of pride in doing a job well. Recognize more than you award or compensate.

When This Happens . . .

You understand the importance of motivation and consider yourself a great team motivator. You give individual praise during your weekly meetings. You bring bagels and juice every Friday when your team exceeds results. Now you are noticing the bagels and juice are becoming routine. One of your coworkers said she is tired of bagels and would prefer if you brought lunch instead. You are thinking that a change is necessary. Perhaps, you will start giving movie tickets to the top performer each week.

Try This

Uh-oh. You are in danger of making the rewards the reason a person does a good job. When you start a cycle of rewarding positive behavior with "things," you are creating a bad habit. It is great to offer bagels and juice—once in a while. Instilling internal feelings of satisfaction are going to last longer. Go back to basics and recognize good performance more than you award it. If your coworkers ask why you are not bringing in food weekly, say "I'll bring something every now and then as a special thank you."

Positive words of encouragement
should be a large part of your vocabulary.

63. Exemplify the Right Behavior

Exemplifying the right behavior should, by now, be your modus operandi. You have learned a lot about shining in your customer service role. When you observe the process, pay close attention to what your coworkers are doing, document both good and poor performance, and positively motivate your team, it is most important that you consistently excel in your own performance to remain a star.

Performance Prompts

- Always act the way you expect others to act.
- Walk the walk.
- Talk the talk.
- Do not expect anyone to do anything you are not willing to do.
- Make customer service crucially important to you. If it is important to you, it will be important to your coworkers.
- Your coworkers need to see that you truly believe your customers are your most important asset.
- No talking negatively about or laughing at your customers. Such behavior gives others the green light to do the same.
- Never become complacent. Always look for ways to improve your performance.
- Remember that your coworkers are your internal customers. Treat them the way you expect them to treat external customers.
- Talk to your coworkers respectfully, and pay close attention to their needs.
- Staying tuned in to your customers and coworkers keeps you thinking innovatively. When you do this you will find ways to do things better.

When This Happens . . .

You want to exemplify the right behavior, but you do not want your coworkers to feel you are no longer one of them. They like to joke around a lot, and customers are often the subject of their jokes. You want to stay friendly with them, yet you understand fully the concept of exemplifying the right behavior. How do you do both?

Try This

You can exemplify the right behavior *and* stay close to your coworkers. It is fine to laugh *with* someone, but it is never okay to laugh *at* someone. If you laugh *at* your customers, other people may think you laugh *at* them as well. People will respect you more when they see that you never make jokes *at* someone else's expense. Stay friendly with your coworkers by staying interested in them. Also, pay attention to your own conduct, and analyze how you behave with your coworkers. Make sure you are not acting as though you are better than they are. You might also ask a trusted friend or coworker how you are being perceived.

Never be above doing any job. Pitch in and help.
This is the best way to exemplify the right behavior.

CHAPTER 10

FEEDBACK
Rave Reviews and Poor Reviews

"I'm not sure that I deserve it,
but I will do my best so that you won't regret it."
—PENELOPE CRUZ

After Bob's meeting, you and the other cast members find it easy to stay motivated. Bob's upbeat comments made all of you feel good, and you continue to give your all every night. After tonight's performance, Bob asks you to stay for a meeting. Hmm, you wonder, what's going on? "Thanks for staying. I've been noticing a change in your performance that I want to discuss with you." This doesn't sound good, you think. "For the past couple nights, when you scream out your lines in the argument scene in Act I, the pitch of your voice raises so much that it's hard for me to understand what you're saying." Raising my pitch?, you silently repeat in a defensive tone. "Sometimes when we act in a long running play, we think our performance is consistent, when in fact we sometimes introduce minor changes that can affect our performance. This happened to me once, and I have a suggestion that I think will help." Maybe I have been raising my pitch, you ponder. What he said makes sense. "You know, Bob, now that I'm thinking about it I can see what you're saying. I've been trying to make sure I'm loud enough, and when I start screaming louder, my voice pitches higher." Bob nods. "I've noticed that you're talking faster and that's when your pitch becomes higher. I think if you slow down your speech, your pitch will lower. Try practicing it before tomorrow night's performance. I'm sure this will help you, just as it did me." Great idea, you mentally agree. "Thanks for the suggestion. I'm going to try it as soon as I get home."

This meeting went well because Bob chose his words carefully. Imagine, instead, if Bob said something like, *Your performance has been slipping. Your pitch is going way up, and no one can understand a word you're saying.* Because Bob was specific in describing the screaming scene, empathized, offered a solution, and gave his assurance, the meeting ended on a positive note.

It is easy for actors to develop bad habits. Unless directors give feedback to their cast members, they cannot expect the actors to improve on their own. Actors need to know what skills are needed to improve their performances. It is the director's responsibility to provide focused, specific, and timely feedback.

As a customer service star, your responsibilities include providing meaningful feedback to your coworkers. Positive feedback reinforces skills, while corrective feedback is the starting point for changing bad habits and poor behavior patterns. The only sure way to continue to give exceptional customer service is to communicate with your coworkers. Discuss what is great and what needs to be improved. As the star of your own performance, you also need to accept feedback graciously from others so that your skills improve as well. When you learn to give—and get—feedback, you strengthen your star power by interacting successfully with your coworkers and ensuring that customers consistently receive high-quality service.

"If you can do what you do best and be happy, you're further along in life than most people."

—LEONARDO DICAPRIO

64. Meaningful Feedback Is Focused, Specific, and Timely

Giving feedback can be challenging if you are not accustomed to doing it. After all, you need to share your observations about someone else and evaluate that person's performance. Although you might think that you do not have the right or desire to do this, you need to take responsibility for giving feedback. Such feedback should compliment your coworker for successful behavior and provide concrete suggestions for improving areas of weakness while maintaining your coworker's self-esteem. Your first step in this process is understanding the components of meaningful feedback.

Performance Prompts

Focused Feedback

- Focus on one area at a time.
- Focus on the behavior, never on the person.
- Begin feedback with *I noticed* or *I observed,* rather than with *You did.*
- *You* statements put the other person on the defensive.
- *I* statements pave the way for honest dialogue.
- When giving feedback, stick to the details, and refrain from being judgmental.

Specific Feedback

- Give feedback only on behaviors and events you personally observed.
- Describe specifically what you observed.
- Tell what impact your observation had on you. *I thought that comment to your customer was great,* or *If I were the customer, I would have been upset by that comment.*

Timely Feedback

- When you need to give feedback, do it immediately.
- Do not postpone feedback, thinking a bad situation will improve on its own. It will only continue or worsen.
- Focus on the present, and avoid mentioning things that happened in the past.

When This Happens . . .

You feel good motivating your team. It is easy to pump up your coworkers by telling them what a great job they are doing collectively, but is it really your responsibility to give personalized feedback to individual coworkers?

Try This

Of course it is! It is everyone's responsibility to give feedback. Think about this: giving meaningful feedback is often a great motivator. Wouldn't you want someone to tell you if you were doing something either incorrectly or in an outstanding manner? Remember, the way you give feedback is very important. Learn to use feedback as a motivational tool, and you will be seen as a caring customer service star.

Good feedback is focused, specific, and timely.
It is also fair, honest, behavior related,
and it encourages open communication.

65. The Wrong Way Demoralizes

You have most likely experienced the following at work. Someone reams you out in front of your peers. Ouch! Even if the criticism is legitimate and even if you are not exactly being reamed out, you do not like hearing negative feedback in front of anyone else. Such an approach leaves you less receptive to corrective feedback. Also, you have most likely felt uncomfortable witnessing someone else receiving negative feedback in front of you. How, when, and where you give feedback is crucial to its acceptance. Make sure you never demoralize anyone when giving constructive feedback. Choose your words, as well as your place and time.

Performance Prompts

- Never discuss a coworker's poor performance in earshot of others.
- Never say *you always* or *you never* when giving feedback. The other person is only going to focus on *always* or *never* and not on the situation you are discussing.
- Choosing words that denigrate and demoralize can zap your coworkers' moods quickly.
- Never give feedback based on hearsay.
- Sometimes it is better to take a *watch-and-see* approach before giving feedback. You might just uncover underlying causes for the behavior that help you understand the situation better.
- Never give corrective feedback without allowing the other person to respond.
- Never give feedback when you are angry or emotional about the situation.
- Never have a closed mind when giving negative feedback. Doing so might prevent you from uncovering the cause of the problem.

When This Happens ...

You are walking to your desk when you overhear one of your coworkers, Zack, talking to another coworker, Allison. "I'm tired of redoing your reports. You always get the total wrong." "I always get it wrong? I don't think so. You don't know what you're talking about." "Yes, I do. I always have to correct your figures." "You do not, and I don't appreciate you talking to me like this." "Just start getting it right, and I won't have to." Zack turns and huffs back to his desk. Allison is so upset she has to take a break.

Try This

Wow. Now that went well, didn't it? Zack is now angrier than when he began his conversation with Allison; she is so upset she took a break; and you feel uncomfortable as a witness to this mess. Think of the things Zack did wrong. He was emotional when he gave feedback; his use of the word always immediately changed the conversation into an argument; he gave feedback in front of coworkers; and he did not give Allison a chance to respond. Make sure you do not commit any of these cardinal sins when giving feedback.

Always think how to say it, when to say it, and where to say it.

66. The Right Way Enthuses

Positively charging people to do their best does not require special skills. It does require awareness, use of positive words and nonthreatening body language, and a sensitivity to appropriate timing. You should determine the best time and place to discuss corrective feedback with others. Choose constructive words, open body language, a time that is conducive to you and the other person, and a place that is private. Once you learn how to give feedback in a positive and constructive manner, you will find that feedback—any feedback—can enthuse both you and the person you are evaluating.

Performance Prompts

- Analyze how you interact with others. Pay attention to the words you choose and your body language. Focus on correcting any of your own behaviors to make sure you come across in a positive and helpful manner.
- Before giving feedback, understand why you are giving it. Make sure your motive is to genuinely improve the situation.
- Before giving feedback, tell the other person what you are going to do. *I'd like to talk to you about something I observed during our meeting this morning. Is now a good time?*
- Find a private place to give corrective feedback. *Let's step outside.*
- When giving feedback:
    - Always state what you observed. *When I began giving my report, you asked me a question before I was finished giving all the figures.*
    - Say how the behavior affected you. *As a result, I lost my train of thought, and it was hard for me to get back on track.*
    - Give the person a chance to respond. *Gee, I'm sorry. I didn't mean to do that. I was afraid if I waited I'd forget to ask.*

- Offer a suggestion or work together to find a solution. *That's understandable. Next time would you mind making a note of your question and asking after I'm done? That would be a big help to me.*

When This Happens . . .

Allison is still upset. You need to talk to her about an incorrect report that she submitted, but you recognize that now is not a good time.

Try This

Wait until she has time to compose herself. "Allison, I need to talk to you about the report you turned in this morning. Is now a good time?" "Sure." "Let's go into the conference room to talk. . . . When I was reviewing the sales figures, I noticed that the daily tallies don't add up to what you show for the total. I had to redo the figures and that caused me to turn in the team report late." Pause. Give her time to respond. "I'm sorry. I get confused with everything I need to compute." Aha. "Let's see if we can work together to find a solution that will make this easier for you." Now choose words that help Allison feel good about herself, and you will enthuse her to do her reports correctly.

Always end a feedback session with words of encouragement and assurance.

67. Quick Feedback Gets Positive Results

When observing your team, look for behaviors and actions that are outstanding, as well as those that need to be corrected. When you focus on trying to catch your coworkers *doing it right,* you are going to find actions to praise. Make notes of outstanding performances, so you can give specific feedback. When you give specific details, good behaviors are more likely to be repeated, and poor behaviors are likely to be corrected.

Performance Prompts

- Acknowledge both outstanding and substandard behaviors immediately.
- Tell your coworkers exactly what you mean.
- It can be a great motivator to give positive feedback in public, but be certain that your coworker is comfortable hearing praise in front of others. It is never appropriate to give corrective feedback in front of others.
- Always make eye contact with the person you are praising or correcting. Make sure your tone and body language fit your message.
- When giving quick feedback, say specifically what you observed and how you felt. *I really liked the way you explained our service charges to that customer. You were thorough and made sure she understood. Great job!*
- Focus on one thing at a time, so your message is not diluted.
- Vary your approach. Do not continue to give quick feedback on the same subject or in the same manner. If you do, you risk sounding shallow.
- Always be sincere when providing quick feedback.
- For those who consistently do things right, continue to offer quick positive feedback. Find ways to motivate and enthuse them, such as giving them additional responsibilities that will enhance their self-esteem.

When This Happens . . .

Today you overhear Zack tell Allison, "You did a great job today." As Zack walks away Allison gives him a quizzical look. Zack was giving quick praise, but *how effective is it to tell someone simply that she did a great job?* Without specific details, how will she know what she did great?

Try This

You also need to give Allison quick positive feedback. Since your conversation about the errors on her report, she has submitted two flawless reports. Not only that, she's turned them in ahead of schedule. "The last two reports you turned in were perfect. I really like the way you now put all the figures in columns. It makes it easy for me to spot individual tallies. Great job on these." Allison smiles broadly. "Thanks. I'm really trying to be extra careful and check my figures." You give her a thumbs up and say, "Keep up the good work." Is Allison more apt to continue to check her figures and put the figures in columns? Because you were specific in your quick praise, she knows exactly what you liked about her work, and she is more likely to repeat these behaviors.

Catching someone doing something right will encourage repeat behavior.

68. Corrective Feedback Changes Performance

By now, you understand how to give feedback. In addition, you have had the opportunity to practice what you have learned. Giving quick praise should be comfortable. When you need to change a behavior or action, give quick corrective feedback and move on. What about those situations, however, in which correcting the behavior requires more than a quick conversation? Suppose that a coworker has a bad attitude toward customers. Suppose you have already given quick feedback on specific observations, but nothing has changed. You see the same poor performance every day. You are beyond the point where quick feedback is appropriate. Now is the time for a corrective feedback session.

Performance Prompts

- Plan your session before meeting with the employee.
- Use your documentation notes to review and refresh your memory.
- Think about how the employee is going to respond.
- When you meet, briefly describe the behaviors you observed.
- Ask the employee to explain. Pause, and give the employee a chance to respond.
- Important: Let the employee do most of the talking, while you do most of the listening.
- From the employee's response, you should be able to determine if the behavior is caused by a misunderstanding (training issue) or by a lack of desire to perform correctly (motivation issue).
    - Training issue: schedule training
    - Motivation issue: the employee needs an attitude adjustment

- Help the employee take personal responsibility for correcting the behavior or action.
- Create a development plan with concrete and measurable goals.
- Finally, state your confidence in your coworker.

When This Happens . . .

On Monday, you trained your team on a new computation method that will give more accurate sales data. After two weeks of flawless reports from Allison, she has started turning in work with errors again. Does she need retraining, or does she not care?

Try This

It is time to plan a corrective feedback session with Allison. After reviewing your notes, plan what you are going to say and think about how she is going to react. Then, meet with her. "Things were going well until training on Monday. Since then, however, your daily reports have had errors." You review the specific errors for each day. "What's going on?" Pause. Now let Allison talk. "I don't know." Pause. Don't accept *I don't know* as a valid response. Wait for her to respond. "I just don't understand the new system. I didn't want to say anything, and I'm sure once I get it I'll do the reports correctly." She is beginning to take personal responsibility. Review the training, and develop a goal plan. "I'm confident that you will take the time to make sure your figures are correct."

Listen carefully to discover the reason for poor performance.

69. Development Plans Set Goals for Improvement

Giving corrective feedback to a coworker is great. Open dialogue often clears the path to improved performance. But how do you make sure the situation is going to improve? You need to take the next step by jointly creating a development plan. To make it easier for both of you, think of a development plan as a goal sheet. You and your coworker are going to agree to concrete and specific goals for improvement.

Performance Prompts

- Before writing the plan, make sure your coworker takes personal responsibility for his improvement. Unless your coworker buys into the plan, it will be meaningless.
- Writing a corrective development plan is a joint project. Unless your coworker takes accountability for the goals, they will be your goals and not your coworker's.
- Before beginning, tell your coworker what you are going to do and why it is important to write a development plan.
- When creating a development plan, include the following details for each area of improvement:
    - Who—is responsible for action
    - What—action will be taken
    - When—action will be improved or completed
    - Where—action will be done
    - How—action is to be accomplished
- When goals are reached, acknowledge and reward accomplishments.
- Even if you or your coworkers do not need to work on specific areas of improvement, everyone should write a personal development plan. Everyone can grow and develop in one area or another, as described in Chapter 3.

When This Happens . . .

After Allison takes responsibility for her development, your next step is to put a corrective development plan into place. Writing goals will help if you are the one responsible for appraising her. When it comes time to write a periodic appraisal, you will have specific details on which to base your judgment.

Try This

"Since this has been an area of recurring improvement, let's write a development plan. We'll set concrete goals for you that will help you steadily improve further. We agreed that retraining will help so we'll include a date for the completion of that retraining. I will take responsibility for training you. Does tomorrow morning at 9 work for you? Great. Let's meet in my office. Once you complete the training, what goals do you want to set for improvement?" "Well, once I understand the material, I'll shoot for 100% accuracy rate on all of my reports. And because of unforeseen delays, how does 98% sound for on-time completion?" "Good. Now we have something to shoot for. I'll follow up and let you know how well you're meeting your goals. We'll work on this together to make sure you're successful."

Writing concrete goals is your first step to reaching them.

70. Periodic Appraisals Are the Most Specific Feedback

If you have not been giving—or getting—periodic appraisals, start now. Appraisals tell specifically how well someone has performed over a designated period of time. Such appraisals should occur at least yearly. People want to know how they are performing and how they are contributing to the overall success of the team and company.

Performance Prompts

- At the beginning of the appraisal period (January, for example), schedule a meeting with coworkers to communicate goals for that period.
- This is a good time to create yearly plans and update goal sheets.
- Include results in all areas in the appraisal process.
- At the end of the period, the goal sheets can be used to compile the appraisals.
- Do not wait until the end of the appraisal period to review results. Results and goal achievement should be discussed regularly throughout the period. In other words, you want to set up your coworkers to succeed.
- Have coworkers review themselves throughout the appraisal period. This encourages everyone to take personal responsibility for goal achievement.
- Create an appraisal framework, a fill-in-the-blank document with goals noted. At the end of appraisal period, you can fill in the blanks with actual results.
- Create a number system that you can apply to each result, such as one to four, to label performance. For example, one = does not meet objectives, two = satisfactory performance, three = more than satisfactory performance, and four = outstanding performance. Use the numbers to average an overall appraisal score.

- Although it is easier to appraise concrete goals, such as sales results or percentage of correct reports submitted, it is also important to appraise subjective goals, such as attitude toward customers based on your observations. Your documentation notes and development plans will support you when discussing subjective measurements.

When This Happens . . .

You have never given appraisals before but you think it is a good idea to begin. It is July, so you plan to wait until next January to start.

Try This

Why wait? Start now. Schedule a meeting with your coworkers to explain that performance appraisals will begin immediately. This year, the appraisal period will be July to December, and yearly appraisals will begin the following January. If you have not done so, write out plans and have everyone set personal goals for achieving specific objectives. Keep a copy for yourself. Be sure each coworker has a copy of his or her plan and goal sheet. Schedule monthly sessions for reviews of individual performances to help every coworker achieve their personal goals. At the end of this year, you will be able to write appraisals based on how well your coworkers achieved their concrete and subjective goals, such as how well coworkers handled customer requests.

The best way for people to know how well they are performing is to tell them specifically how well they are performing.

71. Accept Feedback Graciously

After reading this chapter, you should be on your way to skillfully giving meaningful feedback to your coworkers. The next question is how well do you receive feedback from others? Do you accept it graciously, or do you bristle when someone gives you negative feedback about your own performance? Keep in mind that other people may not be as skilled as you at giving feedback. Learn to accept feedback graciously, and you will improve your own skills.

Performance Prompts

- It is important that you know how others perceive your actions and behaviors.
- Be proactive, and ask for feedback from others.
- You may want to begin by asking a trusted friend or coworker to provide realistic and unbiased feedback.
- When asking, be specific about the skills or behaviors on which you want feedback.
- When someone gives you feedback, listen without interrupting, disagreeing, or explaining.
- Thank the person, no matter how the feedback was delivered.
- Ask for clarification, if needed, and recap what you heard.
- Do not defend or rationalize your behavior. Rather, say that you understand what the other person is saying.
- If appropriate, wait to respond. It is fine to meet later to discuss the feedback. Analyze the feedback before deciding whether to accept it.
- Be open to feedback. View any feedback as useful information.
- Use feedback to create your own development plan, and ask your manager for help or advice when appropriate.

- Learn not to take negative feedback personally. Now that you have a good idea how to give feedback, use those same principles when receiving feedback.

When This Happens . . .

Eric stops you on your way to lunch. "I didn't appreciate the way you talked to us during the meeting this morning. I think this whole appraisal deal stinks. And that goal sheet you had me write? I've been working for this company for four years, and I think I know how well I'm performing."

Try This

Your first instinct is to rationalize why you came up with this new appraisal plan. Don't. Eric is upset, and he will not be receptive right now. Rather, say "I appreciate the feedback, Eric. Are you saying you didn't like the way I told you about the plan or that you don't like that we're starting an appraisal plan?" "I'm no kindergartner. I'm really teed off that you think we need to be appraised." Aha. "OK, I understand how you feel. Why don't the two of us talk about the situation this afternoon?" Now you have time to analyze Eric's feedback and think about how you want to respond.

Before responding to negative feedback, put yourself in that person's shoes. You will have a better understanding of that person's motivation. This will help you to respond appropriately.

CHAPTER 11

MEETINGS
On-the-Spot Rehearsals

"I never felt settled or calm.
You can't really commit to life when you feel that."
—ANGELINA JOLIE

Bob schedules a meeting and explains that Ann has recovered from her broken leg and will be rejoining the production. Although Liz has been performing beautifully in her absence, Ann will be resuming the role. Bob wants input from everyone about how to handle her return, so he opens the meeting by saying, "I'm happy to announce that Ann will be returning next week. I'm also sad to announce that Liz will not be playing the customer service role after Ann's return. I want to solicit ideas from each of you on how we can make the transition seamless. Who wants to go first?" Isabelle speaks up. "Can't you keep Liz in the role? Ann's been out so long she may not be able to fit in." You counter, "That isn't fair to Ann. She was cast for that role, and it wasn't her fault she had an accident." Bob quickly steps in. "Look, Ann is coming back, and she is going to resume her role. There's no question about that. What I want are ideas on how to make this change go smoothly." Once Bob redirects the discussion, the cast members know exactly what he wants, as well as what he does not want to hear, and they begin offering suggestions. As they speak, Bob writes all the suggestions on an easel. "We'll need to rehearse with Ann before she goes on." "Maybe Liz can stay in the role while we bring Ann up to speed." "Yeah, and then maybe for a while Liz and Ann can alternate nights until Ann feels comfortable." "What about keeping Liz in the role permanently a couple nights a week?" Bob notices that Mitch hasn't said anything. "Mitch, what are your thoughts on this?" "Well, I can't tell you how much I appreciated the help I got when I needed it. I think we owe Ann the same. Liz was hired as an understudy, and I think we're going to send mixed messages if we ask Ann to share the role with Liz. I don't think that would be fair to either one." Bob adds Mitch's comments to the easel. "OK, now let's discuss each suggestion and see if we can agree on how to best handle this."

Bob did a lot of things right before and during his meeting. He called a meeting to discuss a potential problem so the group could come up with a plan. He led the meeting effectively and kept everyone on track.

Customer service stars also use meetings to motivate coworkers, to train individuals, to resolve conflict, to solve problems, and to make team decisions. Running meetings effectively includes planning, leading, maintaining control, encouraging group discussion, and ending in a way that energizes everyone attending. Learn how to run effective meetings and you will shine.

Meetings keep people informed and informed people are better able to do their jobs well. As a customer service star, you should keep yourself and your coworkers informed. Everyone will benefit, especially your customers. You will stay a step ahead of any problems, thereby continually providing great customer service.

"But these things, you stick with them, work with them, and they bubble up again, eventually."

—JODIE FOSTER

72. Plan Productive Meetings

You have surely been to meetings that waste your time, meetings you had no need to attend. You wondered why you were there. Or, perhaps, you did have a reason to attend, but the meeting was unsuccessful. Possibly the leader was ineffective, lacking in control, or unprepared. Or, the attendees got off track. Or the issue was not resolved. All of these are time wasters. Never schedule a meeting unless you have a good reason. When the meeting is your responsibility, plan carefully so that you do not waste your coworkers' time. When coworkers take time away from their busy schedules to attend your meeting, be sure you know the who, what, where, when, and how of a productive meeting.

Performance Prompts

- Productive meetings are based on good preparation:
  - What: Decide the purpose.
  - Who: Decide who (and only who) needs to attend.
  - Where: Decide on the location.
  - When: Set the date and time, then notify the participants with the details, including the purpose for the meeting.
  - How: Prepare an agenda to keep everyone on track.
- Only call a meeting for a good purpose and a specific reason. Examples of good purposes are to solve problems, plan projects, train, motivate, present ideas to gain support, and make decisions.
- Plan the meeting location by considering the size and layout of the room needed, what electronic equipment/outlets you will need, the acoustics, the seating plan, other equipment (easels, white boards, etc.) needed, and housekeeping items, such as bathroom locations, break times, and what refreshments, if any, you will provide.

When This Happens . . .

You are a member of a customer service task force that meets weekly. You groan when you look at your calendar for today. You have too much work pending to waste time at another meeting. You would not mind attending if something was accomplished, but nothing is ever resolved. The purpose is supposedly to come up with ideas to improve customer service, but the leader is an ineffective meeting planner. She never has an agenda and never provides a focus for the team. As a result, the meetings are disrupted by side discussions and members who get off the subject. Rarely is there agreement on customer service improvement plans.

Try This

Why continue to go? If you regularly attend meetings that waste your time, consider making the decision to stop attending. First, though, prepare your reasons for not wanting to attend and discuss them with your manager. If your manager is the one running the meetings, you will have to continue attending, although you can tactfully share your feelings and offer suggestions to make the meetings more purposeful and productive.

Never be guilty of wasting other people's time.

73. Lead Meetings Effectively and Efficiently

After carefully planning a productive meeting, think about the best way to lead it. If it is a training meeting, you will have a lot of involvement and will do most of the talking. In a problem-solving or decision-making meeting, your most effective role will be facilitating and guiding the discussion. If you call a meeting to gain support for a change, you will need a persuasive, but conversational, tone, and you will want to hear your coworkers' opinions. Thinking about how you will lead your meeting will enable you to run it effectively and efficiently.

Performance Prompts

In any meeting, you will want to:

- Open the meeting
    - Welcome the group, and clearly state the purpose of the meeting.
    - Start on time. Do not wait for latecomers.
    - Foster a relaxed, neutral atmosphere.
    - Establish ground rules for the meeting: round robin discussion, questions only after your presentation, brainstorming session, and so on.
- Lead the meeting
    - Stay focused on the agenda items.
    - Acknowledge each member's input and allow all members time to speak.
    - Keep notes or write suggestions on an easel or board.
    - Test possible solutions, and work for group consensus.
- Gain agreement
    - When you see members moving toward consensus, summarize accomplishments.
    - Gain agreement from specific members for commitment for future action.
    - Schedule a follow-up meeting if necessary.

When This Happens . . .

Your manager is in charge of the customer service task force meetings, so telling her they are counterproductive and a waste of time will not fly.

Try This

Before meeting with her, think about what you want to say. Stating that you do not want to attend her meetings because they are a waste of your valuable time could very well be a career buster for you. Rather, try a helpful approach. "Can we talk about the task force meetings? I have some suggestions that I think will help the group stay focused. . . . I feel that we keep getting off track and that we don't accomplish our goals. Could you give us an agenda of the items we need to discuss at the beginning of each meeting? That would help us know exactly what issues we are working on. Then if someone gets off track or side discussions start, we can bring everyone back to the agenda. Also, it would help us prepare for next meeting if you could summarize who needs to do what before the next meeting." By providing specific examples in a positive and helpful tone, you come through as interested and caring.

The first item on any meeting agenda should relate to customer service.

74. Sound Questioning Techniques Keep You on Track

Questioning techniques are crucially important to meetings. Poor questions can lead to poor participation, as well as to confused and distracted attendees. More significantly, poor questions can lead to incorrect solutions. Asking good questions helps encourage participation, guide the direction of the discussion, and reach agreement. When planning your meeting, note questions you want to ask and check them off as the meeting progresses.

Performance Prompts

- Encourage participation:
  - Ask the group for their input and ideas about the situation. *Let's see what we can come up with. Who wants to go first?*
  - Give each attendee equal time to participate. *What are your thoughts on improving customer service, Mary?*
  - Value all responses and make a note of them. *I've got some great ideas written on the easel. What else can you think of?*
- Guide the direction of the discussion:
  - Ask specific questions to keep the discussion focused on the main issue. *What are some things we can do to make our customers feel welcome?*
  - Keep the group interested by asking open questions to obtain ideas and closed questions to obtain details. *I like your idea. Can you give us an example of when and how you would do that?*
  - Keep the discussion moving forward so all members contribute. *Let's get back on track. What other ideas do you have about _____?*
  - Test the group to see how well you are communicating. *OK, let's review what we have so far. I want to make sure we have the same understanding.*

- Clarify to reach agreement:
  - Work toward group consensus. *That sounds great. How should we implement this?*
  - Before adjourning, gain agreement. *How do the rest of you feel about the proposed solution?*

When This Happens . . .

At the beginning of your next customer service task force meeting, your manager distributes agendas. You notice, however, that she does not guide the conversation by asking questions. The group starts moving off track, and some of the members are talking among themselves.

Try This

Although your manager is leading this meeting, take responsibility by helping her out. Be tactful, so you do not appear overbearing or trying to take control. "We seem to be getting off track here. Elena gave us an agenda so let's get back to it. She asked for our suggestions and ideas on how we can make customers feel welcome when they come in. Mary gave a great suggestion. What other ideas can we come up with?"

Use positive words and tone when phrasing questions.

75. Maintain Control During Your Meetings

Any star in the role of meeting leader is distinguished by an ability to control the proceedings. If you lead by overcontrolling, attendees will view you as overbearing—as someone who wants to get a point across without any regard for your coworkers' input. If you lead by undercontrolling, attendees will view you as weak. Knowing how much control to maintain is one of the most important components of running a successful meeting. You need to determine how much control to maintain, as this differs for different types of meetings.

Performance Prompts

- When planning a meeting, decide how you are going to control the conversation and discussion, questions, suggestions and ideas, moving through the agenda, and reaching agreement.
- When opening your meeting, let the members know how the meeting will be run; that is, whether it will be an open discussion, a brainstorming session, or one person presenting the information with a Q & A session afterward.
- No matter the format, establish a ground rule to respect each other.
- Maintain control through tactful and positive words and tone.
- When one person is talking, do not allow someone else to interrupt.
- Stop side discussions as soon as they start.
- Do not allow one person to dominate. Interrupt tactfully, and guide the discussion back to the agenda.
- Make sure everyone has equal time to participate.
- Include those who do not participate by asking for their opinion.
- Make sure that each agenda item is discussed fully before moving on to the next.

- Know when to move to the next item. Stop before overdiscussing an item.
- If there is conflict between two or more members during a meeting allow everyone to state their point one at a time; show respect to the speaker; do not judge until they have heard all sides; if possible, allow the group to reach consensus; and, if you make the final decision, explain the reasoning behind your decision.

When This Happens . . .

After last week's meeting, Elena thanked you for helping her out. You casually mentioned something about the importance of keeping control and hope that she got it. At the beginning of this week's meeting, Elena brought the group up to date by stating what you agreed to do to make customers feel welcome. She asks how it is working out. Patrick shares his experience. And then he shares another. You look to Elena. Patrick is long winded and likes being in the spotlight. Is she going to lose control again?

Try This

Elena waits for Patrick to take a breath and says, "Thanks, Patrick. I can see you have a lot of good ideas to share. Let's hear from someone else. Who wants to go next?" Yea, you silently cheer. Elena got what you said about controlling the meeting.

Know when to let the line out and when to reel it back in. That is effective control.

76. Strengthen Group Discussion by Understanding Group Dynamics

Meetings should always include group discussion. Whether you hold a training meeting at which you do the majority of talking or an open brainstorming session to come up with ideas about how to improve customer service, always plan and allow the group to discuss the agenda items. Understanding group dynamics will help you enhance your ability to lead, facilitate, and take part in effective group discussions.

Performance Prompts

- Try to plan an ideal number of attendees for your meeting. If the number of attendees is too small, you might not gain the depth of discussion needed to reach agreement. If the number of attendees is too large, the members may form subgroups or and take sides. Think about what works and what does not with your group.
- In any group, norms will emerge. Norms are the acceptable behaviors by the group members. People who deviate from the accepted norms will usually be dealt with through peer pressure. Someone who repeatedly delays the meeting by arriving late might be given a project no one else wants to do. Someone who sits in the wrong spot might be expected to move. Learn to recognize your group's norms, as well as how they deal with people who deviate.
- Norms may often include a pecking order within the group. Understanding personalities and the pecking order will prepare you to interact well with your group.
- Observation skills will help you understand your group's dynamics. Pay attention to details. Know when to talk, when to listen. Know who talks, know who listens. Pay attention to nonverbal communication. Watch for agreement and consensus before moving on.
- Groups are most successful when members are allowed to actively communicate with each other. Allow your mem-

bers adequate time for free flow of thoughts and ideas. Allowing all members of the group time to talk gives each member a sense of autonomy and control.

- One of your ground rules should always be that members must be respectful toward each other. When you do this, you foster an open, honest, and trusting environment.

When This Happens ...

Now that Elena is leading and controlling the meetings more successfully, she is encouraging open discussion. Unfortunately, Patrick still wants to get on the soapbox. Even when Elena requests other people's opinions, he tries to dominate the meetings. The group is getting tired of his behavior and decides to do something about it.

Try This

This is an example of group norms in action. Patrick is crossing the boundary of acceptable group behavior. You and your team agree to tell him that the group decided to limit comments to twenty words or less. You plan to say it as a joke but still make your point.

Understanding your group's dynamics helps you interact with them effectively.

77. Conclude Meetings by Energizing Your Team

You can do a great job of planning, leading, controlling, and encouraging group discussion during your meetings, but do you know how to end them? If you allow a meeting to just fizzle out, you will lose your impact. If you take a hard line approach, everything positive that occurred during the meeting will be overshadowed by the way in which you ended the meeting. Follow the tips below, and you will end your meetings in a way that leaves your team feeling positively charged.

Performance Prompts

- When you plan your meeting, always plan how to end it. Include an end time in the agenda you distribute at the beginning of your meeting. Be sure everyone knows how much time to plan for the concluding discussion.
- When it is getting close to ending time, start summarizing what was accomplished.
- Discuss what was agreed to in a positive and upbeat manner.
- Even if you did not accomplish all your goals, thank the group for the items they did complete.
- Review individual and group commitments and the action to be taken. Agree to a completion date for each item.
- Review what needs to be done before your next meeting, if applicable.
- Thank the group for attending. Say something to energize them before adjourning. *You did a great job coming up with a solution!*
- When preparing meeting minutes, bring members up to date. For each agenda item discussed, include the major points of the discussion and how the issue was resolved; for open items, include who, when, and how each will be handled. Distribute the minutes as soon as possible.

When This Happens . . .

Patrick gets on his soapbox during this week's meeting. Someone says, "Patrick, it's time to come up for air and let someone else talk. From now on twenty words—or less!" Everyone laughs on cue. Patrick's deviation from the norm was handled through peer pressure, and he does not talk during the rest of the meeting. You notice that after the comment, Elena paid close attention to Patrick, who appears upset. She is now summarizing the meeting and getting ready to adjourn.

Try This

Elena thanks the group for the progress made, and then she says, "Before we leave, I think we need to address what you said to Patrick. I apologize for the group if we offended you in any way. I'm sure what was said was meant as a joke, although it is important that we respect each other since we have a time commitment for our meetings. It's important that everyone has the opportunity to share ideas. I want each of you to make sure that everyone has a chance to contribute. Today we made great progress and I know by next week you will have many success stories to share. Thank you!"

Respecting each member's feelings helps energize your team.

78. Customer Service Meetings Keep You Focused

You should hold meetings for various reasons, including to motivate, train, resolve conflict, solve problems, or reach decisions. No matter why you lead a meeting, always relate your meeting content to your customers. Better yet, plan customer service meetings. Periodically call a meeting at which you motivate your team to give exceptional customer service or at which you solve a problem that is keeping you from giving exceptional customer service. When you hold meetings about your customers, you demonstrate to your coworkers that the customers come first.

Performance Prompts

When holding a customer service meeting, follow this framework:

- Ask a customer service question to get everyone focused.
    - Relate a situation in which you were treated poorly as a customer. Ask what your coworkers would do if they were the employee.
    - Describe a scenario, and ask everyone how they would handle it.
- Motivate your team.
    - Tell your coworkers specifically what they are doing right with customers.
    - Recognize individual performance.
    - Reward team performance.
    - Give team members time to recognize each other.
    - Set new and innovative goals for improving customer satisfaction.
- Solve customer service problems.
    - Clear up confusion when your coworkers handle customer requests in different ways.

- Cover the results from customer surveys.
- Discuss any procedures that need to be changed with regard to customers.

When This Happens …

You are in charge of team meetings and feel you handle that role well. You keep your team informed and work to resolve problems and conflict efficiently and effectively. You do not see the importance of holding specific meetings on customer service.

Try This

What business are you in? Is it the customer service business? If you answer yes to that, the importance of periodic customer service meetings should be very clear to you. Try scheduling a monthly meeting, using the framework above for your meetings. Start by asking a customer-focused question and allow everyone to answer. Getting everyone talking customer service sets the tone of your meeting. Next, motivate your team by recognizing individual and team performance. Motivation gets everyone pumped up. When you are ready to find solutions to problem areas, your coworkers will be in the right frame of mind.

Keep exceptional customer service on everyone's mind by continually talking about it.

79. Contribute Positively When You Attend Meetings

You have learned how to plan and lead a meeting, while maintaining control, fostering open-group discussion, and concluding the meeting effectively. Most likely, however, you will attend meetings a lot more than you will run them. When you attend a meeting led by someone else, you can either be a booster or a detractor. Learn the prompts below, and develop the reputation of someone who is a positive influence during meetings.

Performance Prompts

- Plan to arrive to the meeting before the scheduled start time. You can always bring work to do until the meeting gets underway.
- Show respect to the person leading the meeting, as well as to the other attendees.
- Treat the meeting leader the way you want to be treated when you lead a meeting.
- Read the agenda, and think of ways in which you can contribute. Adhere to the agenda during the meeting.
- Do not get involved in side discussions.
- If you are slated to give a presentation, be well prepared.
- Contribute to the meeting in a positive and constructive manner—and only in a positive and constructive manner.
- When contributing, stick to the point and say what you have to say in as few words as possible.
- This is someone else's meeting and not the time to get on your soapbox.
- This also is not the time to be argumentative or confrontational. Rather, talk to the person in private if you have a concern.
- If other people start getting off track, help the meeting leader get everyone back to the issue under discussion.

When This Happens . . .

During today's customer service task force meeting, Chad, who is sitting next to you, starts whispering while Elena is talking. "I'm bored and I'm getting hungry. Want to go to lunch when we get out of here?"

Try This

Lunch sounds good, but now is not the time to plan. Replying to him would be inappropriate. Ignore Chad, but if he continues whispering to you, send a signal that now is not the time to talk about lunch. Turn your chair so your back is to him. Or turn your head away. Or give him a look that conveys that you are not going to answer him. Whatever you do, do not get involved in a side conversation with him during the meeting. It would show disrespect to Elena and your other coworkers.

When you respect others, they are more likely to respect you.

CHAPTER 12

CONFLICT
Every Production Has Turmoil

"I quit, and then I started again, and then I quit, and then I started again."

—BRAD PITT

Trouble is brewing. Since Ann returned to the production three weeks ago, the cast has divided into two factions. One side is loyal to Liz; the other to Ann. The once agreeable group of actors now has a hard time talking to each other. It all started after Bob's meeting to discuss how to handle Ann's return. Bob explained that Ann had the right to resume her place in the play. It was agreed that Liz would perform for the first week until Ann became acclimated. Once Ann took over, the side supporting Liz started grumbling among themselves. They became more determined to make things difficult for Ann. The side supporting Ann did all they could to help the transition go smoothly. You are afraid the conflict has grown to the point where the audience will notice something is wrong. After tonight's production, Bob asks all of you to stay. "I've been noticing what's going on since Ann returned. We need to discuss and resolve the conflict before things get worse. Ann and Liz, since this conflict involves you, I want you to stay, even though it may be uncomfortable. We're a united group, and I'm sorry to see that Ann's return is pitting actor against actor. It's clear that one group is supporting Ann and the other is supporting Liz. Let's talk this out and resolve our differences before our performances begin to slip."

Because Bob paid attention to his cast, he noticed right away that conflict was arising among his cast members. He did not take a wait-and-see approach. Rather, he decided to get everyone involved to work toward a positive resolution. Bob's goal is to have the cast reach a consensus and make a decision everyone can accept.

No cast is immune to conflict. Likewise, no group that works together is immune to conflict. Whenever people spend a lot of time together, whether they are a cast of actors acting in a play or they are a group of coworkers working together as a team, problems are going to arise. Conflict is often viewed as a bad thing, but it is actually how conflict is handled that can be bad. Conflict, when handled well, as Bob is doing, can be good for a group. It can clear up confusion, channel positive energy, boost confidence, and improve the cohesiveness of the team members.

Some people do not know what to do when confronted with conflict, so they ignore it. Ignoring conflict will never make it go away. Instead, ignoring conflict allows it to fester and grow uncontrollably.

As a customer service star, you need to take responsibility for resolving conflict. If you do not, your customers will notice. The only way to consistently provide the best customer service is to lead a cohesive and undivided team. Learn how to confront conflict and resolve it quickly and effectively. As a result, your team will stay united and strong.

"When you have to cope with a lot of problems, you're either going to sink or you're going to swim."

—TOM CRUISE

80. Conflict Is Good

Conflict is good? Yes, conflict is good. Without conflict, people become bored, complacent, or stagnant. With conflict, people have the opportunity to grow and develop. Conflict may arise when there is poor communication, a misunderstanding, or a disagreement among people. When handled poorly or ignored, the relationships of those involved will continue to deteriorate, leading to poor decisions, tension, and a complete breakdown in communication. When handled in a positive manner, conflict resolution can strengthen relationships, increase productivity, enthuse people, promote the flow of new ideas, and increase understanding and knowledge.

Performance Prompts

- Conflict is a normal component of relationships and should be welcome. In very productive teams, conflict often arises when people are creative, productive, and feel passionate about their work.
- Effective conflict resolution releases pent up emotions, such as anger or jealousy, which strengthens relationships.
- Effective conflict resolution gets people back on track, which increases productivity.
- Effective conflict resolution opens the door to the process of creative thinking, which enthuses people.
- Effective conflict resolution clears up confusion, which promotes the flow of new ideas.
- Effective conflict resolution paves the way to improved communication, which increases understanding and knowledge.

When This Happens . . .

As team leader, you communicate with your group daily; lead your group by modeling correct behavior; foster a supportive environment; work to maintain a cohesive team; observe what is going on; provide feedback that is focused, specific, and timely; and hold regular meetings to solve problems, train, and keep everyone motivated. You feel you are doing everything right, yet you become aware of a conflict within the team. Whenever you are away, you ask Dave to take over as team leader. He is the top performer on your team, gets along well with everyone, and is respected by the group. He is your obvious choice to step up as team leader. Lately, you noticed some of your team members making comments behind his back. Today, you heard someone make a snide comment to Dave about not pulling his share of the work. You know he does more than his share and cannot understand why the group is turning on him.

Try This

You feel uncomfortable about this situation. If you side with Dave you may further alienate your team. You could rotate everyone on the team to be team leader, but you decide Dave is the top performer and deserves this reward. You have two choices: ignore the comments and hope they go away or deal with the conflict. What do you think will happen if you ignore the comments?

View every conflict as an opportunity to improve and strengthen relationships.

81. Communication Is Key to Resolving Conflict

Miscommunication is often at the root of conflict, so it makes sense that good communication is the key to resolving it. You have already learned the principles of good communication. In conflict resolution, it is important to listen, pay attention to nonverbal messages, ask good questions, think before responding, choose your words carefully, say something to show you value those involved, and add charger words to your vocabulary.

Performance Prompts

- Listen carefully before attempting to resolve conflict. Do not interrupt when someone is telling you about the conflict. Listen to all sides.
- Pay attention to nonverbal messages you are receiving—and sending. Maintain a stance that displays you are listening. Show concern in your facial expressions, but do not frown, laugh, or send any improper messages.
- Ask questions to enhance your understanding of the conflict. Use nonjudgmental words when asking. Remember, you are looking only for additional information.
- When you are confident you have enough details to work toward resolution, take the time to think before you respond. Plan what you will say.
- Choose your words—and your tone—wisely. Make sure what you say matches the tone in which you say it. Remember that as facilitator, you want the parties involved to work toward an agreeable resolution.
- Always include a message that shows you value those involved. Displaying empathy is a great way to communicate this.
- When meeting to resolve conflict, incorporate some charger words. *I'm glad you thought of that. Let's try it. How can I help? How can I/you/we correct this?*

When This Happens . . .

You consider your two choices about Dave. If you ignore the comments, the conflict will not go away. In fact, the team may lose its cohesiveness. You really have only one choice. You must deal with the conflict. You have heard team members making snide comments about Dave. You heard one of them make a comment directly to Dave. Do you have enough information to know how to resolve this issue?

Try This

No way. You heard some comments, but you do not know the root cause of the problem. Before you can plan how to resolve this conflict, you need to meet with each person individually to get a better understanding of what is happening. Start by relating what you heard, and ask what is going on. Listen carefully. Pay attention to body language. Ask questions until you are sure you understand the root cause. Let everyone know this issue is important to you and that you are going to work to resolve the problem.

Listen carefully to your coworkers, understand them, and respond to them.

82. Anticipate Problems and Deal with Them Immediately

Conflict is not going to dissolve on its own. Someone must take ownership of each conflict and work to resolve it positively. There is another element of conflict resolution—the time factor. Once you become aware of a conflict, you do not have the luxury of time to wait and see what will happen. It is imperative that when you see a problem developing, you deal with it immediately. Become an active observer and communicator in order to anticipate problems as they are arising. With this approach, you will be able to resolve conflict when it is still in the formative stage.

Performance Prompts

- Always look for things that are amiss, such as people who have different points of view, do not agree with a decision, or feel unfairly treated.
- Ask team members, coworkers, and friends to tell you when problems are arising.
- Before initiating any project or program, develop a contingency plan. Watch for any problems that may develop and be ready to implement your contingency plan.
- Before initiating any action, review past projects and programs, analyze what conflicts occurred, and how they were resolved.
- Confront conflict as soon as you notice it. Never let conflict grow into an unmanageable situation.
- Before plunging in to resolve the conflict, take time to think about it.
- Plan the best way to handle the situation. If the conflict is between two people, you most likely do not need to involve your entire team in its resolution.
- Think about how the involved people are going to respond when you meet. Who will be confrontational? Who will be passive and give in?

- If you do not know how to resolve the conflict, ask for help.
- Ask your peers how they effectively resolved conflict on similar problems.

When This Happens . . .

You noticed the conflict, and you must deal with it. You now have enough information from your individual discussions to plan your group meeting. The problem is that you like everyone on your team. This puts you in an uncomfortable position.

Try This

Get past feeling uncomfortable. You have a problem, so deal with it. This does not mean you need to jump right in. First, carefully plan how you will work to resolve the conflict. If four members of your team are involved, meet with those four only. Think about how you are going to open the meeting and facilitate the discussion. It is very important that you also think about how each team member is going to respond. Who will be outspoken? Who will try to dominate the conversation? How is Dave going to handle a meeting where others may criticize him? By carefully planning, you will find the best way to resolve the situation.

When you meet conflict head on,
you will gain respect as an involved leader.

83. Find Win-Win Solutions

How well did you resolve a conflict if one or more of the involved parties do not feel the outcome is acceptable? Not well at all! Unless all involved members feel satisfied with the solution, you are not going to be successful in resolving the conflict. Your main goal should be to resolve conflict by finding a win-win solution, one in which everyone feels valued.

Performance Prompts

- Open your meeting by explaining that this is a solution-seeking meeting. Leave complaining at the door!
- Make sure all involved people are present at your meeting.
- Your role is to facilitate the discussion and guide your coworkers to reach consensus. Describe the problem, and ask for ideas to resolve it.
- Allow everyone time to talk. Listen to each suggestion, and note all ideas.
- Stay focused on the issue at hand. No name calling, using *always* or *never*, or ganging up on someone.
- Consider all ideas. An idea that sounds silly may be the right solution.
- Analyze the consequences of each suggestion.
- Work toward consensus and a solution that everyone can buy into. Complete agreement may not be possible, but try to find a solution that is acceptable to all.
- If tempers flare, take a cooling-off break.
- The best solution for right now may be to rest the problem. Adjourn the meeting, give everyone time to think, and then meet again.
- If you cannot reach consensus as a group, you may have to make the final decision as the group leader. Take your time before deciding, and explain why you are making this decision.

When This Happens . . .

You set the meeting time and state the reason for it. Before the meeting, talk to everyone, individually, to explain the ground rules.

Try This

By explaining the ground rules before the meeting, you accomplished one important goal, that is, you set the tone for the meeting. You open the meeting by saying, "I value each of you, and I appreciate how closely we all work together. When I noticed a problem, I felt we needed to resolve this right away. Each of you has explained why you're upset that Dave is acting team leader. I've talked to Dave to get his input. The main problem is that when Dave takes over as team leader, the rest of you have to cover his workload and that puts a burden on you. Let's come up with some ideas to solve this. Who wants to go first?" You facilitate the discussion and guide your coworkers toward an acceptable solution. They support Dave as acting team leader. They decide that they can handle his work one day a week, but if Dave is team leader more than that, he will have to take responsibility for doing part of his workload. They will work as a team to distribute and take responsibility for his work. Everyone accepts this win-win solution, and you feel that working together on this has strengthened the team.

People feel empowered
when they are a part of the solution.

84. Turn Chronic Complaining into Contentment

Do you know anyone who is a chronic complainer? Of course you do. It might be a disgruntled coworker or a coworker who tells you about every personal problem. It might be a customer who tests your patience repeatedly. You try to be nice, to listen and accommodate the chronic complainer, but it is starting to bring you down. People generally do not complain constantly. Something specific may have happened to cause this behavior. Constant complaining may be caused by unhappiness over a particular situation, a feeling of being treated unfairly by another person, or a feeling of not having any control over a situation. By talking it over, you can work to resolve the conflict.

Performance Prompts

- Analyze what is going on. Try to figure out why the person is complaining.
- If you cannot figure it out, put yourself in the complainer's shoes. You might understand the reason if you see things from the person's vantage point.
- Think about what you want to say when you meet with the person.
- Think about how the person is going to respond.
- When you meet, explain how the constant griping makes you feel. You may also want to share how you think it must make the complainer feel.
- Display empathy. Stress that you want to be supportive and help resolve this.
- Ask what is going on that is causing the person to constantly gripe. What is causing the unhappiness?
- Listen carefully. Let the person vent. Ask questions to uncover the reason.
- Ask what the person can do to change the situation. Ask or say how you can help.
- Agree on what needs to change to stop the complaining.

- Follow up, and pay special attention to the person and situation.

When This Happens . . .

You are close to your customer, Janice, and are her main point of contact in your company. For the past month or so, she has developed a negative attitude toward your company. It started out with minor complaints, but lately she complains about everything. She complains about your products, about your delivery time, about your billing system, and even about being put on hold when she calls.

Try This

After thinking over the situation, you wonder if Janice is upset about something you did. Do more than wonder. Talk to Janice. "Janice, we've always had a great relationship. Lately I've noticed that you seem unhappy. That isn't like you. Something is upsetting you and that's upsetting me. I'm wondering if I did or said something to offend you. Please tell me what's going on." Janice assures you that she likes dealing with you, but she does not like dealing with your coworker in another department. He talks down to her and makes her feel as though her business is not important. She is thinking of changing companies. "I am sorry. I had no idea. We greatly value your business and here's what I'm going to do. . . ." Talking it out not only shows Janice that you truly care about her, you demonstrated your willingness to help change this situation.

Focusing on the solution
helps you overcome any problem.

85. Turn Problem Performers into Peak Producers

Dealing with a problem performer can be unnerving. If you have already provided sufficient training and given corrective feedback, but the problem continues, you are probably dealing with a problem performer who is not motivated to perform the job properly. Unless you turn this behavior around, the situation is not going to correct itself. Here is more bad news. Your coworkers will lose respect for you as a leader if you do not handle the problem performer. To correct poor performance or change a poor attitude, deal with the situation right away, and deal with it head on.

Performance Prompts

- Plan your meeting. Think of questions that will help uncover the reason for the behavior.
- Picture how your coworker is going to respond. This is a touchy situation; you may be dealing with someone's bad attitude. What is the worst case scenario?
- When you meet, remind your coworker that you already discussed this issue.
- Ask your coworker to explain why the problem has continued. Be direct and to the point when asking for an explanation.
- Listen. Let your coworker do the talking. Resist guiding the conversation.
- Ask questions to uncover the cause of the poor performance and bad attitude (don't like my job, don't like talking to customers, unhappy about something).
- Gain agreement that the person knows the correct behavior. State that the incorrect behavior is unacceptable. Focus on the behavior only, not the cause.
- Ask what your coworker is going to do to change.

- Discuss and agree on the resolution. Keep the monkey on your coworker's back.
- Write an action plan and review the steps necessary to reach the objective.
- Affirm your confidence in your coworker's ability to change. Follow up.

When This Happens . . .

During your corrective feedback meeting with Ian about the tone he was using with customers, he said he did not know what to say to customers who were upset and maybe that is why he sounded sarcastic. You went over a scenario where a customer was angry and coached Ian how to speak in an appropriate tone. After your feedback session, you heard from a coworker that Ian made a sarcastic comment about you. You shrugged off the comment as Ian's way of venting and saving face. This morning you overheard him being sarcastic when a customer asked a question.

Try This

Ian is a problem performer. After planning your meeting and thinking about how Ian is going to respond, you meet with him. "Last week we talked about the tone you were using. You said it was because you didn't know what to say when customers were upset. You agreed to change, yet this morning I heard the sarcastic tone when a customer asked for help. Please explain." Agree that Ian knows the correct behavior. "You agree that you know how you should speak to customers." Get Ian to take responsibility. "This is unacceptable. What will you do to make sure this doesn't happen again?" State your confidence. "I know you will turn this around. Our customers deserve to be treated well."

Changing behavior happens only when the person sees the need to change.

86. Remain Calm and in Control at All Times

There will be times when you will be so upset about something, you will feel ready to blow. There will also be times when an angry or upset person who is ready to blow approaches you. When either of these situations happens, use all of your self-control and inner strength to make the situation better, not worse. Put your positive attitude to good use; do not turn negative when you—or someone else—is upset.

Performance Prompts

When you are ready to blow:

- Breathe slowly and deeply. Consciously focusing on your breathing can help slow your racing heart and racing thoughts.
- Count to ten. Get away from the situation. Take a short break or go for a walk.
- Never lash out at anybody when you are angry. No one will come away with positive feelings when you are unable to control your emotions.
- Always think before you speak. Do not say something you are going to regret.
- Never, ever threaten anyone. Walk away from a situation if you feel you are losing control of your emotions.
- Learn not to take anything personally. Always try to understand why someone has acted inappropriately before talking to the person about the situation.

When someone else is ready to blow:

- If an angry person approaches you, let the person vent. Do not make the person angrier by not taking the time to listen.
- Always remain patient, calm, and in control when listening and responding to someone who is angry or upset.

- If the person appears to be losing control, stay composed and speak in a calm voice. *You are really angry now. Let's take a walk so you can compose yourself. When you can talk about this calmly, I'll do everything I can to help you.*
- If someone is speaking or acting inappropriately, focus on the behavior and say why it is inappropriate. Assure you will help. *Please stop yelling. Customers might hear you and that is unacceptable. I'm going to help you.*
- If someone threatens or intimidates you, ask for help or get away from the situation. Go immediately to your manager and explain what happened.

When This Happens . . .

Your customer, Taylor Davis, comes tearing into your store. He looks ready to blow and is heading your way. As he reaches your desk, he pounds on it and screams, "You told me you would reverse this charge and you didn't. You must be a moron!" Your heart races, you are taking shallow breaths, and you are unnerved.

Try This

Calm down, and control yourself. He yells, "You said you'd take care of it!" Take a deep breath. Speak slowly, quietly, and calmly. "Taylor, I'm really sorry. It should have been processed before your bill date. Please have a seat and let me find out what happened. I will make sure this is taken care of right away for you."

By staying calm, you help the other person calm down.

CHAPTER 13

COMMITMENT

Take It from the Top

"You've achieved success in your field when you don't know whether what you're doing is work or play."

—WARREN BEATTY

Successful directors know that to consistently receive rave reviews, they need to constantly improve the skills of their actors, as well as their own skills as directors. Bob grew and developed his skills throughout the run of the play. He also worked to improve the skills of his cast. After a rough start as director, Bob learned to communicate well with the actors throughout the run of the play. He worked with the cast and rehearsed until they were ready for opening night. He dealt with change by being proactive and having a contingency plan. He developed a spirit of teamwork and camaraderie among the actors. He was a hands-on director who observed the process, and he provided specific and focused feedback. He held meetings to keep the cast informed, and he dealt with conflict by working to resolve it successfully. After a long run, tonight is closing night. You are all ready to celebrate. Bob thanks all of you for your award-winning performances; they are what kept the play running as long as it did. "I don't want anyone to feel sad about the play coming to an end. Rather, I'd like each of you to challenge yourself to continue to improve your skills and also to help others improve their skills. Look for opportunities to grow and develop. Who knows? One of you might direct a play that I'll be in. I'd be proud to work with each of you again. Now, let's celebrate."

Directors understand that when the run of a play ends, they need to begin planning for the next play. It is easy for employees, managers, and owners, whose run has no end, to become mired in the day-to-day grind and lose their focus on the future. When you learn to look forward to and plan for tomorrow, for next month, for next year, you will have a higher chance for success and a brighter outlook.

Now, it is time for you to commit to your role as customer service star. You are the director—of you. No matter what role you are cast to play, whether it is to interact directly with customers, to manage customer service employees, or to own a company, you are your own director. You are the manager, the president, the CEO of you. You can be a star if you choose to be. It is entirely up to you. Only you can make your choices. Only you can manage your behavior and attitude. How do you measure up? Remember that in life you play many roles and you can be a star in each role. When you are at work, get fully into your role, play it to the best of your ability, and let your star shine.

When you commit to do your best every day, you will keep your forward focus. You will look for innovative ways to keep the momentum going, seek learning opportunities, develop the ability to be proactive rather than reactive, and strive to nurture and improve customer and coworker relationships. Most importantly, when you develop an attitude of gratitude, you will find inner peace, contentment, and happiness. When you do these things you are a superstar, no matter what role you are cast to play.

"The only failure is not to try."

—GEORGE CLOONEY

87. Keep the Momentum Going

It can be tough to keep the momentum going, especially when you are already working efficiently and effectively. When you reach the point where your days become routine, it may be difficult to maintain focus. The danger is that routine can become mundane and thereby lead to boredom. Keeping the momentum going, however, can be done with careful planning. Create a development plan for yourself and help your coworkers understand the importance of creating one for themselves. When you do this, you will find ways to keep your job and workplace exciting and interesting. Not to mention yourself!

Performance Prompts

When you are still working efficiently and effectively, it is time to create a new personal plan. Ask yourself:

- What can I do to improve my communication style?
  - How well am I communicating to others?
  - How effective am I in sending verbal and nonverbal messages?
  - How good am I in tailoring my messages to the person with whom I am communicating?
- What skills do I need to develop to improve and strengthen myself?
  - What can I do to make myself better?
  - What classes can I take to continue my self-development?
  - What projects/assignments can I volunteer to be involved in?
- What role do I play on my team, and how can I improve it?
  - How do I add value to my team, my company, and my interactions with customers?

- What interpersonal skills do I need to develop or strengthen?
- What can I do to help others succeed?

- What support do I need from others?
  - Have I developed the alliances that will help me?
  - Have I developed a relationship with a mentor?

When This Happens . . .

You just received your appraisal, and you feel great. Your manager gave you the highest rating for every objective. You appreciate the rating; after all, you worked hard to achieve this level of performance.

Try This

Think it is time to rest on your laurels? NO! You reached your company goals and objectives. You feel confident you will continue to perform at this level, yet there is always room to grow. Analyze areas that could be improved and create a personal plan to continue to develop your skills. Take a class, and learn a new skill. Join a community group, and volunteer your time. Read a self-help book, and apply the knowledge you learn. Mentor someone else. Look for ways to continue to become a better version of you.

What was outstanding yesterday may only be mediocre today, not good enough tomorrow. Always look to improve.

88. Stay One Step Ahead of the Crowd

Along with keeping the momentum going, you also want to stay one step ahead of the crowd. How do you accomplish this? By seeking ways to continually learn. Learning should never stop. You learn something and then things change. You must learn something new or learn the old in a new way. Develop your desire to become an active learner. Also develop your desire to become an active teacher. Learning, as well as teaching, is a lifelong process.

Performance Prompts

- Knowledge truly is power.
- View every day as an opportunity to learn something.
- Set a goal to learn one new thing every day.
- When you approach every day as an adventure, it makes it easier to find that one new thing to learn.
- Look for opportunities to learn from every person you encounter. Do not discount anyone, especially children.
- Become a continual learner by taking a class, even if it is a class just for fun.
- View every learning opportunity as an opportunity to improve yourself. Even if you think a class you must take is going to be boring because you already possess that knowledge, try to find one thing you do not already know. Learning even one new thing can make the entire class worthwhile.
- When things do not go your way, and you are forced into a new situation, look at the situation as an opportunity to learn new skills.
- Always question the status quo. Find ways to make things better, even if they are already pretty good.
- Look for things that need to be changed, especially those things within you.

- Watch for bad habits that are forming, and do something to change them.
- Share your knowledge with others.

When This Happens . . .

After receiving your outstanding appraisal, you are feeling good about your performance at work. You wish others on your team would perform at the same level.

Try This

Why not share your secrets with your coworkers? Or with your customers? Find ways in which you can teach others the things about which you are knowledgeable. Perhaps you created a question framework to use as a guide when you take calls from customers. Show it to your manager, explain how it helps you, and volunteer to share it with coworkers. Perhaps you receive numerous calls from customers for technical help with one of your products. Talk to your manager, and volunteer to write a help sheet to give to customers when they purchase this product. Always look for opportunities to learn and also to share your knowledge with others. Become not only a continual learner, become a continual teacher.

Strengthening others
helps you strengthen yourself.

89. Pro-Act, Don't React

Are you proactive or reactive? Think before you answer. Being proactive is more difficult than you might imagine. Do you have emergency plans in place? Or do you wait for an emergency to move into crisis mode? If so, you will react to the situation in a manner that may not be the best. We tend to think of crisis situations as circumstances that affect many people. Most crises, however, occur on a much smaller scale. At work, a crisis might be something as simple as how to handle the workload when a coworker calls in sick. When you plan proactively, you will have contingency plans in place. You will also look for opportunities to actively change situations before they become emergencies. And, if an emergency occurs for which you have no plan, your proactive state of mind will help you manage the crisis more efficiently.

Performance Prompts

Before a crisis:

- Be on the lookout for things that need to be changed, improved, or eliminated.
- Always have a contingency plan in place for emergency situations.
- Also have an emergency plan for disasters or other unforeseen events, both at work and at home. Make sure everyone involved knows their role before an emergency happens.
- Practice your contingency plans with everyone who might be affected. Remember the fire drills you did in school? There was a good reason for those drills. Make sure you and your coworkers practice your own "fire" drills.

During a crisis:

- Number One Rule: Remain calm. You will not do anyone any good if you lose your composure.
- Take a deep breath. Or a few.
- Figure out how much time you have before you must take action.
- You may not have time to carefully think out your plan of action, so put your critical thinking skills to good use.
- When time permits, ask others for their ideas and help.
- Think of the worst case scenario for the action you are choosing.
- Help others remain calm by modeling calm behavior.

When This Happens ...

Your longtime customer just called to tell you his company will not be renewing their contract with you. They found another vendor with a larger product selection and a faster delivery time. This is a huge account, and the loss of revenue is going to greatly affect your company's profits.

Try This

Do you have a contingency plan in place for these types of events? In business, nothing is certain, and this is one area in which you should have a plan. Your plan might be to try to win this customer back by offering an incentive. Or it might be to maintain enough accounts so that the loss of any one will not be devastating and create a crisis.

In business, as in life, nothing is certain.
Always plan for the unexpected.

90. Create Creative Coworkers

You already learned about developing a cohesive team of coworkers. You know you are maintaining a cohesive team when goals are achieved, team members respect each other and work well together, progress does not slow when one member is away, and morale and commitment remain high. Where do you go from here? You are the energy booster for your team. Think of yourself as a coach and a cheerleader.

Performance Prompts

Hand out positive charges every day. Positively charging your coworkers encourages them to be creative.

- Keep a smile on your face—a genuine smile.
- Be sure to use positive words and open, relaxed body language.
- Maintain a high energy level.
- Make sure you are sincere in everything you do and say.
- Ask for suggestions and input from your coworkers. If you cannot act on their suggestions, explain why in an encouraging manner.
- Tune in to creative ideas, and encourage coworkers to develop these ideas.
- Get to know your coworkers, so you will know how to respond to their needs.
- Expect everyone to be supportive toward each other.
- Continue to spend time with your team, to focus on open communication, to attend team meetings, to strive for cooperation, and to maintain an environment that encourages creativity.
- Catch your coworkers "doing it right" and offer heartfelt praise.
- Mistakes are often borne out of creativity. Learn to let go and give coworkers the opportunity to do it their way, even

if they are going to make mistakes. Channel what you learn from the mistakes into creative thought.
- Be consistent with your coworkers. People want to know they can expect the same treatment from you every day.

When This Happens . . .

You have developed your motivational and leadership skills and feel you are doing what it takes to keep your coworkers motivated. Lately, though, you wonder if you are doing enough. Your team seems to be in a rut, and you are concerned that the level of customer service you provide is going to suffer.

Try This

At some point in everyone's career, this is going to happen. Yes, you absolutely may be doing enough, but you cannot do it all. Make everyone responsible for motivating everyone else. Get everyone to work together to implement new strategies for improving customer service. Hold a brainstorming meeting to ask for suggestions and ideas. Encourage everyone to be creative and come up with innovative ways to do the old things in a new way.

Staying tuned in to your customers—
and to your coworkers—keeps you thinking innovatively.
When you do this you will find ways to do things better.

91. Cultivate Contented Customers

Merely meeting your customers' needs is not going to earn their loyalty. Customers also have expectations. They are going to measure your company, not by how well you meet their needs, but by how well you exceed their expectations. You must continually look for innovative and creative ways to improve in order to build a customer link for life. To achieve this, you must continue to maintain a high level of efficiency and effectiveness. Customers will not stay loyal if you sacrifice efficiency and effectiveness for the sake of being creative and innovative. Strike a balance between the two, and you will find the secret of cultivating customers who remain contented and loyal.

Performance Prompts

- Building loyal relationships with customers is your key to business success.
- The only sure way to keep customers is to provide the best customer service every day.
- Tell your customers you appreciate them. Better yet, show them.
- Start thinking like your customers. Who are they? Why do they come to you? How do your products and services help them? What can you do to improve?
- Customers define what it takes to make them happy. Ask your customers to define this for you.
- Make it easy for your customers to do business with you. Review all policies and procedures. Ask your customers what you can do to improve.
- Treat customers the way you expect everyone in your organization to treat them.
- Building your customer base is important, but your existing customers should always be your number one focus. It costs a lot more to develop new customers than it does to keep existing ones.

- Customers can be your best marketing tools. Make sure what they are saying about you is helping your business.

When This Happens . . .

Recently your company began a campaign to increase your customer base. You are offering rebates, discounts, and incentives for first-time customers. This is great, and you are gaining new customers.

Try This

These are all great marketing tools to bring in new business. Now it is important that you do something special for your existing customers, so they know they are also important to you. Schedule a customer appreciation day or week. Provide food, hold a special drawing for them, or give something to each of them when they come in or call. If this will not work for your business, find a way to show and tell your customers that you value their continued business. Your number one goal should always be to keep your existing customers contented and happy.

Find new ways to keep your customers WOWed.

92. Develop an Attitude of Gratitude

Do you know that if you change the way you look at the world, the world will change the way it looks at you? Think about that question for a moment. How you see yourself has a direct effect on how you see the world and how you present yourself. How you present yourself to others directly correlates to how others are going to respond. You have probably heard some version of the story about the man who was nearing a city he had not been to before. He met an old man sitting by the side of the road and said, "I've heard the people in this city are rude and inconsiderate. Is this true?" The old man replied, "Yes, you will find the people here rude and inconsiderate." A while later another man approached the city; again, he had not been there before. He said to the same old man, "I've heard the people here are warm, friendly, and helpful. Is this true?" The old man replied, "Yes, you will find the people here warm, friendly, and helpful." The moral of the story is obvious. If you expect negativity, you will receive negativity, and if you view the world from a positive frame of mind, that is how the world is going to respond to you. What you send out is what you are going to get back.

Performance Prompts

- When you train your mind to think thankful thoughts, your self-talk will be more positive. Be thankful for everyone—and everything in your life.
- Be thankful for every role you get to play. Strive to be a star in each role.
- When you are grateful, you will send out positive and uplifting messages.
- When you send positive messages, you will feel genuinely happy.
- Developing an attitude of gratitude enables you to feel happy and contented. It also makes it almost impossible for you to feel unhappy or discontented.

- And yes, you can be happy and content and still have goals for bettering yourself and your life. Being contented does not mean you are complacent. Making yourself better is going to increase your attitude of gratitude.
- Strive for your goals—and—continue to be grateful for what you already have.
- When you develop your attitude of gratitude, share your appreciation for others. Tell people you are grateful for them.

When This Happens . . .

Some people see the cup half full, while others see it half empty. If you are one who sees it half empty, you may not understand this gratefulness thing. When you focus on the negative and things that go wrong, you will block grateful thoughts.

Try This

Everyone has things that go wrong, yet some people are able to take things in stride while others consider every wrong thing as an excuse to be unhappy. If you do not already possess the attitude of gratitude, it is going to be difficult for you, but you can develop this quality. Start by changing your self-talk. When you find yourself becoming negative, STOP! Think about someone or something good in your life. Say *Thank You*—and mean it. Change your self-talk, and change you. You can do it if you want to do it.

A grateful spirit = a great-ful spirit
full of happiness and contentment.

93. Make Fun Time a Daily Goal

Life is an adventure. Why not make the adventure fun? As you develop your attitude of gratitude, make it a daily goal to have fun. Whether you are interacting with your customers, your coworkers, your family, or friends, look for opportunities. This begins by not taking yourself too seriously. When you take yourself too seriously, you will find things that are wrong and then you will lose your attitude of gratitude. Of course, there will be times in your life when you will not feel like having fun. Also, there are times when it is inappropriate to focus on fun. When life events get you down, it is still okay to smile. Eventually, you will know that you can laugh and have fun again. When you make fun time a daily goal, you will find the world a more fun place.

Performance Prompts

- If you are not having fun, you probably are not completely happy.
- You will be more effective and efficient at work when you enjoy working.
- View each day as if it were the first day of a new job, even if you have been doing the same one for a long time.
- What is the one thing you are really good at and love to do at work? Find ways to do more of it.
- What is the one thing you are good at and love to do outside work? Find some way to integrate what you love to do into your job.
- Every day find something to laugh, or at least smile, about. Learn to laugh at yourself, but never at others.
- Enjoy life's simple pleasures. The best part is that most of them are free.
- Schedule fun time every day, whether it is lunch with your coworkers, a ballgame with your kids, or a quick phone call to your best friend.

- Stay fully involved in what you are doing. Enjoy the present.
- Find reasons to celebrate, and celebrate in style.
- Break the routine by breaking one bad habit. Replace it with a good one.

When This Happens . . .

You have been doing your job for a few years now and frankly, it is beginning to be boring. You are thinking about looking for a new job that will be more exciting.

Try This

Finding a new job that is more exciting will most likely be a quick fix, because once you learn that job, it will also become routine. It makes more sense to explore the opportunities for incorporating more excitement into your current job. Think about your strengths and what you love to do. Do you like to write? If so, look for opportunities. Volunteer to write a training package or a company newsletter. Like to teach? Volunteer to train new employees or work with customers when they purchase a new product. Find some way to integrate what you love to do into the job you have. If you cannot find any way possible to showcase your talents at work, volunteer in your community. Find an outlet to do what you love to do. When you do this, you will be more content and satisfied with the job you have.

Having fun makes everything more pleasurable.

CHAPTER 14

QUICK TIPS

Cue Cards

"Life is very interesting . . . in the end, some of your greatest pains, become your greatest strengths."

—DREW BARRYMORE

Even when directors spend the time necessary to thoroughly rehearse with their actors, they know that rehearsals alone may not be enough to get through the complete run of a play. Actors can flub, whether it is opening night or the one hundredth performance.

As a customer service star, you may face the same challenge. Even when you take enough time to learn how to do your job, there are times when you need a quick fix, a quick learning tool, or an attitude adjustment to reinforce previous training, to stop bad habits from becoming routine, or to boost your morale.

Cue cards are quick learning tools and attitude adjustors that you can use to help keep yourself and your coworkers on track. Cue cards are effective for the obvious reasons: they are quick, they are targeted, and they are to the point. You will find these cue cards effective because they are easy to learn, easy to remember, and easy to share with your team.

Use these cue cards when you need a quick fix or an attitude adjustment. They are learning and teaching tools that will boost your confidence and help you be your best. That way you will be able to consistently provide your best customer service. Post the cues in the workplace, make up cards for coworkers to keep on their desks, reinforce them in meetings, or put your imagination to use to find fun ways to incorporate them into your workday.

"If you want a happy ending, that depends, of course, on where you stop your story."

—ORSON WELLES

94. CHARACTER Counts

When you have character, you care about yourself and about others. When you develop a positive character, you will feel better about yourself, and you will enhance your relationships with others.

- **C-ommitment**
    - Give each day 110%. Show that you are dependable and willing to give more than expected. Work toward finding positive solutions.
- **H-onesty**
    - Always tell the truth. Honesty builds trust, which builds loyalty, which brings success. Always act ethically; do the right thing.
- **A-ppreciation**
    - Look for the good in other people. Show your sincere gratitude. Make others feel they matter and are important to you.
- **R-espect**
    - Hold other people in high regard. Recognize the value of others and be polite, patient, and positive.
- **A-wareness**
    - Turn your care and concern outward to other people. Be genuinely interested in those around you. Pay attention to pick up on cues. Also be aware of the image you are projecting.
- **C-ompassion**
    - Show your concern by enhancing your understanding of other people. Walk in another person's shoes. Empathize.

- **T-olerance**
  - Everyone has the right to their opinions, goals, religions, lifestyles, and so on. Rather than judging people who are different from you, accept their differences. Always accept others for who they are.
- **E-ncouragement**
  - Be an inspiration and motivation to others. Show people you care. Help others feel good about themselves. Go the extra mile. Think of ways to help.
- **R-elationships**
  - Everything you do in some way affects someone else. Always think of the impact of your actions. Connect with people on a close level and form the bonds that develop into special relationships.

95. CHANGE for the Better

Life is all about change. Nothing stays the same for very long. When you learn to look change in the face and work through the process, you will find it easier to embrace change. Learn to help yourself so you can help others.

- **C-ommunicate.**
  - Clearly communicate the vision, goals, and rationale for the changes. Be available. Listen carefully. Ask more questions. Get others' opinions and reactions to the changes. Strive to be specific, candid, and objective.
- **H-elp.**
  - Look for opportunities to help others work through the change process. Tell others you want to help. If you cannot help immediately, schedule a specific time when you can. Do more than you are asked to do.
- **A-nticipate.**
  - Watch, look, and listen for things that seem to be wrong. Set up early warning measures to help you know when problems are arising. Fix the issue before it turns into a major problem. Review your work plan for each goal, and ask yourself what can go wrong as we work through the change? Incorporate contingency plans to avoid a crisis situation. Discuss issues with your coworkers. Have an answer for every *what if* you can think of.
- **N-urture.**
  - Nurture yourself and those around you while you work through the transition period. Be more patient. Do not expect more than you can realistically expect. Share your needs with others, and encourage them to share their needs with you. Stay tuned in to your coworkers during the time of turmoil.

- **G-o.**
  - The change is here, and there is no turning back now. It is more important than ever to display a positive attitude about the change. Remain sincere and objective, not phony and overly optimistic. Tell others exactly what is expected of them. Talk about the change in more concrete terms. Do not dwell on what used to be.
- **E-nthuse.**
  - Encourage and reward others for embracing the change. Recognize achievement. Ask for and act on suggestions for improving your workplace and organization. Be a quick change artist by enthusing and energizing those around you.

96. LISTEN UP for Better Communication

The secret of being a great communicator is to listen a whole lot more than you speak. Whether you are communicating with customers, coworkers, or other people, be the best listener you can be.

- **L-earn.**
    - View every listening experience as an opportunity to learn something.
- **I-dentify.**
    - Look for ways to identify with what you are hearing.
- **S-ay nothing.**
    - Keep quiet and listen.
- **T-une in.**
    - Give your full and undivided attention to the speaker.
- **E-mpathize.**
    - Put yourself in the speaker's shoes, and show understanding and empathy.
- **N-o judging.**
    - Remain neutral while you are listening to the message.

- **U-tilize** the information you received to prepare your response.
- **P-ause** before you answer. Always think before you speak.

97. CARE About Your Customers

It is human nature to want to be noticed and recognized by others. We all want to hear a word of encouragement, to know we are needed, and to know others care for us. How do you show your customers you CARE? By communicating, acknowledging, responding, and encouraging them. Do these every time you talk with your customers. Reinforce customer care when you train, hold meetings, or resolve conflict with your coworkers. When you demonstrate that you care for your customers, you motivate your coworkers to care for them.

- **C-ommunicate** openly and honestly with each customer. Communication is the foundation on which strong relationship are built. Listen actively to the person with whom you are communicating. Focus solely on that person, and shut out everything else. Show you are interested in communicating with that person only. Think before you speak, and choose uplifting words. Words, once spoken, can never be taken back, so think before you speak, and ask yourself how will what I say sound to my listener? Ask good questions. Maintain a cheerful and enthusiastic attitude. Be aware of your nonverbal communication, and maintain an open, relaxed, and confident demeanor. Ask yourself: am I doing all I can to communicate clearly?
- **A-cknowledge** what your customers are saying to you. Stay tuned in, and stay interested. Show compassion for them. Watch for nonverbal signals that might not match what customers are saying. Acknowledge what you pick up from the nonverbal signals. Ask yourself: do I acknowledge each customer and give individual attention?
- **R-espond** to customer needs. Give customer problems top priority, and handle them immediately. Find the right solution for each customer. Show and tell your customers that you appreciate them. Thank them for doing business with

you. Ask yourself: am I responding to each customer's needs?

- **E-ncourage** customers by demonstrating that you value them. Tell them they are important to you. Respect their decisions, even if you do not agree with them. Respect cultural differences by being tolerant of all customers.

98. Face-to-Face Customer Service

To customers, you present the face of your business. Build strong relationships with customers by meeting them face to face.

- **F-irst impressions matter**—smile; make eye contact; keep an open, relaxed demeanor; stay interested.
- **A-ttitude is everything**—present a positive attitude; be trustful; be helpful; be credible; believe you can make a difference.
- **C-ommunication is key**—tune in; focus; listen completely; think before you speak; speak clearly.
- **E-ffectiveness is important**—know your products and services well; look for ways to solve problems; find the best solution.

When you put your best face forward, customers will give you:

- **F-eedback**—when you listen, customers will tell you what they need.
- **A-ction**—customers will act on your proposed solutions when they trust you.
- **C-ommitment**—strong relationships equate to committed customers.
- **E-nd result**—when you are effective you will see positive results.

99. Stop! Look! Listen! Act! for Outstanding Customer Service

When you find your level of customer service is derailing, get everyone back on track by remembering to stop, look, listen, and act.

- ***Stop!*** everything you are doing when a customer comes in or calls. Greet the customer. Give your name. Ask how you can help. Form a mindset that this particular customer is the reason you have a job.
- ***Look!*** at the customer. Focus only on the customer with whom you are speaking. Help your customer form a positive first impression of you by making eye contact, smiling when you speak, presenting a positive attitude, being interested, and maintaining an open, relaxed demeanor.
- ***Listen!*** actively and completely. Pay complete attention and really listen to what the customer is saying. Before responding or forming your conclusion, gather as much information as you can to make sure you understand the request. Remain objective and never judge a customer. Listen, also, for what is not said. Pay attention to nonverbal cues and tone.
- ***Act!*** on the customer's request. Think of options to solve the problem, determine the best solution, and present it to your customer. Be prepared to offer an alternative solution if the customer is not satisfied. Next, always do what you say you will when you say you will. Show that you are reliable and accountable.

100. Customer Satisfaction Quiz

After every customer interaction, ask yourself:

- Did I do everything possible to give that customer outstanding service?
- What was the customer's first impression of me?
- How well did I relate to the customer, and did I build a rapport throughout the interaction?
- How well did I listen and understand the customer's request?
- How well did I answer all the customer's questions?
- How well did I handle the customer's request?
- Did I offer the best solution?
- How effective and efficient was I?

If you cannot answer all the questions positively, think about what you could have done differently and next time do it.

101. Customer Quick Bytes

Use these customer quick bytes as meeting openers to generate new ideas or to solve problems.

- Customers will generally remember a company for two reasons:
  - When the product or service is particularly good, or
  - When the product or service is extremely bad.

How are our customers remembering our company?

- Customers appreciate the following qualities in customer service providers:
  - Courtesy;
  - Knowledge of products and services;
  - Reliability;
  - Decision making ability.

How do we measure up?

- The top reasons for customer dissatisfaction are employees who:
  - Ignore customers;
  - Do not listen;
  - Are not knowledgeable;
  - Are not reliable;
  - Do not follow up or follow through.

Which of these are we guilty of?

- Service that was outstanding yesterday may only be satisfactory today and not good enough tomorrow.

What can we do to make sure our service is outstanding every day?

INDEX